WHAT PEOPLE EXPECT
FROM CHURCH

Ministry for the Third Millennium
Edited by Lyle E. Schaller

WHAT PEOPLE EXPECT FROM CHURCH

Why Meeting People's Needs Is More
Important Than Church Meetings

ROBERT L. RANDALL

ABINGDON PRESS / Nashville

WHAT PEOPLE EXPECT FROM CHURCH:

Why Meeting People's Needs Is More Important Than Church Meetings

Library of Congress Cataloging-in-Publication Data

Randall, Robert L., 1942-
    What people expect from church : why meeting people's needs is more important than church meetings / Robert L. Randall.
        p. cm. -- (Ministry for the third millennium series)
    Includes bibliographical references.
    ISBN 0-687-13387-4 (pbk. : alkaline)
    1. Pastoral theology.   2. Mission of the church.   I. Title.
II. Series.
BV4011.R37   1993
253'.01.'9—dc20   92-33162
                                                                            CIP

Scripture quotations are from the New Revised Standard Version Bible, copyright © 1989, by the Division of Christian Education of the National Council of the Churches of Christ in the United States of America. Used by permission.

93   94   95   96   97   98   99   00   01   02 — 10   9   8   7   6   5   4   3   2

MANUFACTURED IN THE UNITED STATES OF AMERICA

ACKNOWLEDGMENTS

For several long years now, my good friends and colleagues in ministry, Larry Randen and Richard Wolf, have read the rough drafts of everything I have written for publication. I thank them again for their usual patience, their critical eyes, and their supportive humor.

I also want to express heartfelt appreciation to Lyle Schaller. His encouragement and guidance have made the writing of this book a joyful experience.

Finally, I'm grateful to be working and worshiping in a church that sustains my soul. Here at St. Peter's I feel understood and come to understand. Here I know I belong and find messages of hope. May these words of affirmation uplift you, dear community, as you have uplifted me.

Robert L. Randall
St. Peter's United Church of Christ
Elmhurst, Illinois

89031

CONTENTS

Contents

6. Teaching That Connects   55

    Creating an Understanding Environment   57
    Expanding Others' Understanding   61
    Supporting Belonging   65
    Instructing for Hope   69

7. Church Administration That Cares   73

    Acting and Programming with Understanding   74
    Anchoring and Opening Others' Understanding   78
    Maintaining Boundaries for Belonging   82
    Mobilizing Hope   85

8. Congregational Life That Embraces   89

    Worship Life   89
    Service Life   93
    Social Life   98
    The Reconciling Life   101

The Leaders Around Jesus   105

Notes   107

Selected Bibliography   109

FOREWORD

The farmer who began a twenty-year nap in 1890 and woke up in 1910 could have gone back to work immediately and functioned effectively with perhaps two or three hours of on-the-job instruction.

The bookkeeper who took a twenty-year nap beginning in 1920 could have awakened in 1940 and gone back to work without learning new skills.

The worker on the automobile assembly line of 1935 could have taken a twenty-year nap and found few changes in that job in 1955.

The parish pastor of 1939 would have encountered few problems, except perhaps for an automatic transmission in that new car, after awakening from a twenty-year nap in 1959 and resuming the parish ministry.

When he awoke from his twenty-year nap, Rip Van Winkle was confronted with both continuity and discontinuity, but the discontinuity was not as pronounced as the continuity.

During the last two decades of the twentieth century, the parish ministry has experienced huge changes. Many of these changes began to surface in the 1950s and 1960s, but their impact was not felt for another decade or two. Among the most highly visible are (1) the erosion of denominational loyalties; (2) the emergence of a rapidly growing number of megachurches with seven-day-a-week ministries; (3) the enhanced vitality, relevance, and numerical growth of scores of large Protestant congregations in the central cities; (4) new approaches to ministries with families that include young children; (5) the frustrations created by increasingly severe economic pressures on the small-membership church; (6) the impact of television on the way information is sent and received; (7) the emergence of a new and different generation of young people born in the 1969–82 era; (8) the proliferation of agencies and institutions, including parachurch organizations, teaching churches, and entrepreneurial individuals, who are offering a growing array of resources to congregations; (9) the expansion of the agenda in theological seminaries so that preparing people to become parish pastors is only one of a lengthening list of responsibilities; and (10) an unprecedented demand by people, especially those born after 1940, for a meaningful teaching ministry that will help them on their religious pilgrimage.

One product of these changes is that the role of the parish pastor is being redefined. To be an effective parish pastor today requires a far higher level of competence than was required for a similar level of effectiveness in 1955.

More important, however, has been the impact of these and other changes on the life of the worshiping community. The congregation that settled down for a long winter nap back in the 1950s or 1960s or 1970s is awakening to a world filled with a huge amount of discontinuity with the past. This is especially relevant for those congregations seeking to reach and serve the generations born after 1955. For this discussion five changes stand out.

The first is the replacement of survival goals at the top of the individual's agenda with the search for meaning, community, and identity. This is described in a wonderful book, *The Identity Society,* by William Glasser (New York: Harper & Row, 1972).

A second and overlapping change has been the replacement of the traditional emphasis in our society on functions, tasks, and assignments with a new focus on relationships. This can be seen in the priorities of the social studies teacher in the local high school, in the criteria for choosing a job or vocation by many in the generation born after World War II, in the advertising of consumer products, and in the contemporary definition of a "good marriage."

A third change can be seen in what church shoppers seek as they search for a new worshiping community. The average size of a Christian congregation in North America, both Catholic and Protestant, has tripled since 1890. The number of megachurches has at least quadrupled since 1960. In a world filled with anonymity, one obvious choice is the small congregation modeled after the television program "Cheers." We all treasure the affirmation that comes when people call us correctly by name, when they are genuinely glad we came, and when we can find comfort in discovering that all our troubles are the same.

But this also is a society that emphasizes quality and has taught people that they have a right to select from among a broad range of highly attractive choices. As the church shoppers search for a new place to worship God, do they choose the intimacy of the small fellowship or the quality and choices offered by a large congregation?

That introduces a fourth change. Today, people expect both-and, not either-or, answers to complex questions. One example is the expectation that every congregation should be able to offer a friendly atmosphere, an affirmation of the importance of one-to-one relationships, a high quality ministry, and a wide array of attractive choices.

Finally, one of the most profound and far-reaching changes reflects who determines the agenda. For generations, authority figures told the people what they needed. Today, universities, automobile manufacturers, grocery stores, hospitals, clothing designers, public schools, and other producers of goods and services have discovered they must be sensitive and responsive to the expectations of consumers.

Among the Christian churches in North America, Catholic and Protestant, this helps to explain why inherited loyalties, denominational allegiance, and geographical convenience are no longer as influential in the choice of a new church home as they were only three or four decades ago.

The seekers, shoppers, and pilgrims of today are looking for a church that can offer them a high quality and meaningful response to their personal and religious questions. They seek a congregation, without much concern about the denominational label on the building, that affirms their relational needs. They seek a church that understands their yearnings.

What are those yearnings? What is the scriptural basis for understanding those yearnings? That is the central theme of this book. How can a congregation, regardless of size, be responsive to those yearnings? That is why this book has been written. How can preaching reach out to those yearnings? How can the teaching ministry connect with those yearnings? How can the life of that worshiping community affirm and embrace those yearnings? Those are the questions Robert Randall addresses in this book.

This is not a book for those who are convinced that what worked in 1949 or 1956 will work in 1999 or 2006. This book has been written to and for those who are open to the challenges that tomorrow will bring. It is not written for those who want to do yesterday over again.

This also is the first volume in a new series on the new realities of being the church in a changing world. This new series is designed for leaders who are at least as comfortable with the new as with the old, who enjoy the challenges of shaping a new tomorrow rather than conforming to the constraints of yesterday, and who are convinced that new wineskins are needed to bring the Gospel of Jesus Christ to new generations of people.

Most of all, this series is directed to leaders who seek to be guided by the needs of people rather than by the survival goals of institutions. Those considerations explain why Dr. Randall's book was chosen to be the first volume of this new series.

Lyle E. Schaller
Yokefellow Institute
Richmond, Indiana

INTRODUCTION:

THE CROWD AROUND JESUS

After Jesus had left that place, he passed along the Sea of Galilee, and he went up the mountain, where he sat down. Great crowds came to him, bringing with them the lame, the maimed, the blind, the mute, and many others. They put them at his feet, and he cured them, so that the crowd was amazed when they saw the mute speaking, the maimed whole, the lame walking, and the blind seeing. And they praised the God of Israel.   *(Matt. 15:29-31)*

The church is a gathered crowd around Jesus. A faithful church, now and into the twenty-first century, knows its identity, and in the deepest religious sense we are merely a crowd gathered around Jesus. We come as a crowd with our brokenness and handicaps, looking for God's healing touch. We come praising Jesus' name for making us well. However organized we might be, however prestigious we might feel, we are nothing more sophisticated than a crowd hungering for wholeness.

We need this crowd around Jesus. We need the actual visible presence of church members gathered in worship, service, and fellowship. In this crowd we can feel ourselves cared for and understood. When the crowd is gathered, the voice of

Jesus is heard and we come to understand more fully. With the crowd we know securely that we belong. Surrounded by the crowd our spirit is infused with hope.

People yearn for this crowd around Jesus.[1] A current novel describes how people still "repair to the church on Sundays." That's an old word, *repair.* It means "to return," "to go often and customary." But the word also catches up the deeper meaning of why people return to church—namely, to feel "repaired," to have the pieces of their lives put back together again. That's the same reason people came to Jesus, to be repaired, to be made whole physically, emotionally, and spiritually. And the way in which people will be repaired now and in the future is no different from Jesus' day. We all feel restored when we gather around Jesus and feel the humanizing presence of one another.

One effort of this book is to provide an orientation for dealing with the central needs of people here at the end of the twentieth century and deep into the twenty-first. Those needs are not functional ones but relational ones. The principal breaks in people's lives are their hearts. Hearts are broken when relationships are broken. People repair to the church looking to be healed. They seek restoring relationships that can soothe them and fortify them for the abundant life Christ would have them live.

More specifically, people enter the church yearning to feel understood. They search for pastors and parishioners who are willing to listen and know what they are going through. They look for someone who can reach sensitively through their "nobody knows me" isolation and touch them.

People turn to the church yearning to understand. They seek meanings that can soothe their fears and give life order. They make themselves receptive to guiding explanations from pastors and lay teachers that can help them find their way through their constantly changing and often ominous world.

People come to the church yearning to belong. They long for the companionship of kindred souls, who can assure them that they are acceptable and not alone. They are eager to be connected to a faith community that upholds values and standards while also affirming that "we're all in it together." People repair to the church yearning for hope. They thirst for visions and stories that confirm the significance of their yesterdays, encourage them to put one foot in front of the other, and assure them that the promises of God will be kept.

The future faithfulness and wellness of congregations rests in large measure on how empathically they recognize and minister to the needs of people. Today, and increasingly in the next century, individuals of all ages will look for a church home that creatively touches their deepest yearnings to feel connected. These yearnings—more than physical proximity to a church, community prestige of a church, denominational loyalty to a church, or family tradition in attending a specific church—will determine where persons choose to worship and serve.

Responding to these needs, however, should not be undertaken as a means of "keeping the church alive." As we enter a new century, perhaps we can be liberated from a pervasive survival anxiety that so badly dominates much of our thinking in the church. Instead, we best respond to persons' needs because Jesus responded to us, and because the Holy Spirit leads us to find new ways of ministering to the old relational yearnings of men, women, youth, and children.

Furthermore, responding to these needs should not be undertaken as a means of preparing for the "real" work of the church, whether that be service to others, evangelism, or church growth. Nurturing the human bonds within the congregation *does* empower the congregation and individual members to extend themselves lovingly to all the world. But the building up of supportive relationships within the congregation is itself the church's mission. It could even be argued that it is the church's primary mission.

Nurturing relationships within the congregation is the dedicated undertaking of many clergy and lay leaders today. That endeavor springs in part from a vision of what the church is as well as from an awareness that people increasingly long for a relational way of life within the church. That endeavor also stems from a need to confront a "functional orientation" toward ministry that can eclipse a ministry devoted to the care of persons.

A functional orientation subtly predominates when a congregation becomes organized around "functions." At times this is a temporary state. One writer spoke of this as the "subversion of the agenda."[2] In general terms, this state can be described as shifting the focus of the congregational agenda from ministry to institutional maintenance. One classic example is when a congregation launches out on a visitation-evangelism effort in order to attract new members needed to help pay for church repairs. Another example is when a congregation adds a new staff member and programming to avoid dealing with the insensitive behavior of a powerful senior minister. Then again, a church that desires to be "the leading light" in the community may proliferate activities primarily to enhance its prestige. Every congregation, small or large, is vulnerable to slipping into this type of functional orientation, especially when hard times hit or the church is moving through a transitional period. In any case, a focus on "institutional maintenance" shifts away from a ministry to persons.

More insidious than this is when a congregation becomes chronically organized around functions. One sign of this functional orientation is the terminology used to describe the church's "business." Pastors and lay leaders talk of *programming activities* for the *membership*. Toward that end, *directors* are *assigned tasks* and given *schedules*. They are expected to arrange *meetings* with other *task force members* to *facilitate* and *coordinate* the activities, and finally to *write up* an *evaluation* of the *success* of the whole *process*.

While no minister may consistently talk this way, this functional mentality is central in many clergys' thinking. One pastor said, for example, "Our staff and programs have developed to the point where I can function as the executive administrator." His secretary was also given a new title befitting the new organizational theme: office manager. More was involved here than simply importing words from the corporate world to speak of the work of ministry. The explicit language reflected the implicit reality of minister and congregation organized around functions. Parishioners sensed this. When one woman told the office manager about some problems she was experiencing, the office manager said she would mention it to the pastor. "Oh no," replied the woman, "he's too busy running the church."

The ascendancy of a functional orientation is indicated also when functioning groups and functioning practices become autonomous, as if they had a life and meaning and purpose all their own apart from aiding struggling souls. For example, certain long-standing committees within the church can obtain a sacrosanct status, where they are deemed inviolable to change or to criticism. Liturgies and rituals can become immutable to alteration, as if power resided in the doing of these acts themselves. Procedures and policies can be responded to as prescribed laws that must not be questioned. Rather than these functions being a means for ministry to people, they become ends in themselves. In the same vein, functions tend to dominate over relationships in the church when the most influential committees are finance and property.

Perhaps the most devastating indication of a functional orientation in a congregation is when people themselves are related to in terms of their functioning rather than in terms of their personhood. This attitude was present in one minister who said about his parishioners, "I want them to know the truth, get on the stick, hop to it, and do it!" The productive performing of truth was more central to him than the people who enacted the truth.

A functional orientation at the expense of relational support is evident in another pastor's stance when he proclaims that,

"The church is not here for the people. The people are here for the church. Our purpose is to worship God, and not to 'cultivate the self' by focusing on 'meeting people's needs.'" People functioning as worshipers is deemed more important than worship functioning to aid people. The pastor apparently forgot the ecclesiastical guidance given by Jesus when he said, "The sabbath was made for humankind, and not humankind for the sabbath" (Mark 2:27).

This functional attitude was also dominant in a pastoral relations committee who regularly reminded their minister, "You're just a hired hand here," and in a church council who declared to their new pastor, "You are here to take care of us; we're not here to take care of you." That same functional orientation is present when potential members are termed "enrollment enhancers," individuals are viewed as "pledging units," parishioners' "attendance" is expected for the success of instituted church programs, members' "compliance" with denominational dictates is covertly demanded, and persons' "affirmation" of the pastor is socially mandated.

A functional orientation ultimately estranges us not only from one another but also from God. Such functional inclinations blunt a sensitivity to, and a reliance upon, forces and energies that emerge as grace moments in people's lives. A focused concern with people and their needs, and a ministry principally organized around supportive relationships, is compromised if not essentially abandoned when a functional mentality takes over.

The crucial point here is not that "functions" within church are "bad" or that ministers and parishioners should not be viewed as called upon to fulfill various "functioning" roles. People can genuinely relate around parish functions and activities. Furthermore, to be committed to a relational way of life within the congregation does not mean rejecting the church's organizational responsibilities. This is not an either-or issue— namely, a congregation is either "functional" in its ministry or "relational." A congregation will inevitably be some mix of each. What is at stake, however, is which one *dominates* in the church: functions or relationships.

This book is directed to clergy and lay leaders of all churches who are committed to the primacy of nurturing and reestablishing relationships within their congregations. Smaller congregations tend naturally to focus on relationships. They complain about the functional orientation of the denomination, but they basically tend to keep the relational dimension of life number one. Having grown up in a rural congregation, however, I know personally how relationships still need to be nurtured there, and how even in a "family church" functions can become the center of effort if not controversy. Larger congregations, on the other hand, are inclined to drift in the direction of functions at the top of the priorities when ordering parish life. Having worked for many years in a large congregation, I am personally aware of the constant need to reinstate the primacy of relationships.

By focusing on relational needs within the church, I do not suggest that clergy or lay leaders should cater to people's whims. Neither do I intend to cultivate a climate of self-absorption, where the congregation becomes a consumer of its own life rather than a contributor to God's wider world. Rather, people can become their fullest selves, and a means of grace for others, as they enjoy loving responses to their human needs. Furthermore, when a congregation acts as a relational community it becomes a sustainable community—that is, it can focus on individual people and individual places while also keeping the regional and global world firmly in mind.

Because some parishioners have desperate needs for relationships, it is possible for congregations to become excessively preoccupied with their relating, to the near exclusion of everything else connected with the role of ministry in the church. This happens, for example, when power struggles between families or groups within the church absorb the majority of their energy. This happens also when meeting at church becomes more important than worshiping there. Members in a small rural parish noted that if it weren't for the coffee hour, people wouldn't come to church at all. It was no surprise, then, when this congregation made sure that the fellowship hall was air-conditioned before the sanctuary. Those of us committed to nurturing relationships within the church would best remember that just as "functions" can become a preoccupation, so also can "relating."

If our commitment is to nurture and reestablish relationships within the congregation, then we must strive to understand what people need in those relationships. We must also be aware of the various levels of these needs and how people respond when their relational needs are not met. Chapters 1 through 4, consequently, speak of people's yearnings to feel understood, to understand, to know they belong, and to garner hope. These four needs are not exhaustive, but they are indelibly central in the lives of those who repair to the church.

The recognition of these core relational needs has emerged from pastoral counseling work with pastors, individuals, and congregations.[3] These pastorally observed needs are remarkably similar in essence to the six spiritual needs of Americans today as found in a recent Gallup poll: (1) the need to believe that life is meaningful and has a purpose; (2) the need for a sense of community and deeper relationships; (3) the need to be appreciated and respected; (4) the need to be listened to—to be heard; (5) the need to feel that one is growing in faith; (6) the need for practical help in developing a mature faith.[4]

Books and articles directed toward religiously sensitive people enjoy mass appeal when they touch on these four cardinal needs. For instance, the tremendous popularity of M. Scott Peck and his seminal book, *The Road Less Traveled,* is based on Peck's acute sensitivity to these needs. Peck empathizes with people who yearn to feel understood. He immerses himself in their difficulties, articulating their struggles and agonizing over them. Peck teaches those who yearn to understand. He opens windows, allows new ways of seeing things, and gives people reason to be proud of themselves as they take up the noble work of self-reflection. Peck connects with people who yearn to belong. He lifts up their shared stories so that they feel the companionship of kindred souls. Peck promises to those who yearn for hope. He massages dry bones with visions of graceful moments that revive our lives.[5] To nourish and restore people, those who write for the public and those who serve in local parishes must speak this language of the heart.

Guided by our understanding of the central relationship needs of parishioners, coupled with an understanding of how congregations can slip into a functional orientation, we then make specific suggestions for how our preaching, teaching, church council administration, and general congregational life can become more deeply personal. We do that in chapters 5 through 8. In short, we (1) broaden our understanding of what is needed in human relationships; (2) remind ourselves of how we can diminish, if not lose, the human touch within our congregation; and (3) consider altered ways of making relationships gracefully incarnate within our community.

Some congregations that have achieved much in functional terms still possess a self-righting capacity. They can be impressed by signs of having shifted away from their central ministry and are able to reorient themselves to their divine calling. That capacity, of course, is the work of the Holy Spirit. It is upon the grace of God that we must ultimately rely as we attempt to become transformed communities—now and into the twenty-first century.

1.

YEARNINGS TO FEEL UNDERSTOOD IN THE CHURCH

A woman found her pastor in the office and began to tell him about her aged mother, whom she was bringing into her home to live. She told of her mother's senile, raging outbursts at her and of the dramatic changes this would mean for her family. Suddenly her eyes filled with tears and she said beseechingly, "Pray for me! But I do love her so!"

This woman was pleading to be understood. She was reaching out, hoping her minister would sense her anguish and be moved to ask God to strengthen her. In addition, she needed him to genuinely understand that she was not complaining. She wanted him to comprehend that love for her mother filled her as much as the heavy burden she was taking upon herself.

People come into the church yearning to feel understood. They bring all their normal needs for feeling understood. They bring all their unfulfilled or crushed needs for being understood. They come hoping that in this place (the church) and with this person (the minister) and with these people (other worshipers) they will find especially resonating hearts. Pastors and parishioners are special figures endowed with assumed compassionate spirits, who are expected to give themselves to others in understanding, caring ways. This is not just the "Pollyanna" attitude of novice churchgoers. In the inner recesses of all people beats the hope that the pastor, the people, and God will be there for them in ways that make them know they are truly known.

The intensity of that need to feel understood varies among people. On the one hand, some people enter the church with normal needs to experience others being sensitive to what they are going through. Having received healthy responses from parents or other significant persons, they come into the church anticipating that they will find additional understanding individuals. They anticipate that these individuals will generally affirm their feelings, give them comfort, and support their values. The church, therefore, is looked upon as an extension of the empathy these people have already experienced and as a haven of understanding when the rest of the world seems insensitive.

When these people experience the failure of others in the church to be understanding of them, they feel hurt. They typically respond with some degree of irritation and/or dismay. These are normal responses by people when their central needs are thwarted. Persons with firm self-esteem do not become unglued by this failure to be understood, however. They are able to maintain their general sense of well-being and their general caring attitude toward others. In addition, the level of their irritation and/or dismay stays within reasonable limits, as does the expression of these emotions to those who have not responded understandingly.

On the other hand, some people enter the church with excessive yearnings to be understood. Persons may expect near-perfect understanding responses from clergy and laity. They may constantly rely on these understanding responses to feel good about themselves or to keep themselves from falling apart. When others in the church fail to provide the understanding these parishioners need/demand, they feel crushed. They react with severe forms of outrage or despondency. They may verbally strike out at others, or they may withdraw from church life altogether.

The needs of people to feel understood by others in the church vary between these two extremes. Likewise the reactions of anger or hurt vary from person to person—and from situation to situation. Whatever the intensity of need may be, people come into the church not as guilty souls yearning to be forgiven, but as sensitive souls yearning to feel understood.

People have always needed to feel understood. That need seems especially pressing today, however. In the first place, it is often difficult to find others who will, or can, listen quietly and thoughtfully. In our functionally oriented society, many individuals are geared more to action of some sort and less to patiently immersing themselves in another's inner world. Even if individuals are care-oriented, they tend to want to "do" rather than to deeply "listen," to "make it better" for another rather than to "feel it" with another.

Furthermore, it is often difficult to find individuals who can tolerate, let alone understand, intense feelings. The very depression or outrage a person hopes to have understood tends to push individuals away. Many individuals fear being dragged down by the powerful emotions people around them express. Consequently, hurting people are often left to handle their problems alone, or they are forced to find those who are suffering similar disturbing experiences. Self-help groups centered around specific concerns frequently develop out of the isolation participants have experienced from the rest of society. Self-help groups can be representative of the absence of understanding, rather than the expansion of understanding, in the world.

As in both the past and today, people in the future will come into the church hoping to find individuals who understand them. They will sense that such understanding is essential to their being healed and remaining whole. While "the need to feel understood" may not be given as an explicit reason for their joining a church, just as it is not today, it will remain the basic yearning of every heart that repairs to the crowd around Jesus.

2.

YEARNINGS TO UNDERSTAND IN THE CHURCH

A young mother, whose baby died mysteriously in her crib, returned to her church's Bible study group. "Why?" she asked them, as she had herself a thousand times. "For what purpose? For what good?" She needed to find some meaning in it all. She needed to grasp an understanding that could erase her pain and help her regain hope.

People come into the church looking for pastors and parishioners who can help them understand. They bring their normal need to continually understand the forces of life. They also bring their lack of understanding and their confused understanding.

People look to the church for understandings that will order their lives. They make themselves receptive to meanings that will grant them a sense of life's regularity and predictability. Sometimes that is the primary reason people yearn to understand: to help them maintain order and equilibrium in their lives. Consequently, they elicit explanations from ministers and respected parishioners that will ease their misery, give reassuring names to their vague fears, or reinstate the trust that their lives are worthwhile. Pastors and parishioners are expected to provide lifesaver wisdom that people can latch on to when they feel confusingly adrift.

People also look to the church for understandings that will transform their lives. Cautiously, as well as courageously, they open themselves to new realizations that can beckon them toward new visions and hopes. They seek alternative explanations about the events in their life stories so that they can see the world and themselves differently.

Once again, parishioners vary in the intensity of their need to understand. Those fortunate enough to be nurtured by guiding parents or other individuals look for the church to support those core understandings they have already learned. Blessed with a firm sense of who they are as persons, they are not in desperate need of new explanations as a way of holding the pieces of their lives together. Their firm identity allows them, furthermore, to risk opening themselves to new, alternative explanations offered by a respected pastor, teacher, or parishioner. When others do not supply adequately supportive understandings, if especially needed, these basically assured people feel some apprehension and increase in tension, but the core of their being remains firm. They search elsewhere for sustaining meanings or recall the wisdom of idealized figures in their past. Their irritation and/or dismay does not prompt them to berate the minister or leave the church.

Persons who have suffered the absence of meaning-giving figures in their lives, however, may look for authoritative substitutes with whom they can merge. Lacking a reliance on their own knowledge and experience, they may adopt the perspective of any willingly available pastor or congregation. The pastor's or congregation's truth, values, and meanings become the content of the empty person's understanding. Not infrequently, these persons demand that others tell them what to do and what to believe. When the offered advice or beliefs fail the anxious individuals in some way, they become more despondent and often enraged. They may then build up walls of protection that resist ideas that are unlike their own narrow ones.

The need to understand exists on a wide spectrum between these two extremes. But anywhere along the continuum, parishioners regularly or intermittently return to the church for understandings that will validate, soothe, or restore them.

Through the centuries people have regularly relied on the church for understandings that could order and transform their lives. That reliance is especially urgent today, and it will be more so in the future. On the one hand, life is becoming more and more complex. The alternatives facing people at each stage of life are increasingly numerous as well as ominous. Decisions that people are forced to make contain broadened potential for good or ill, while at the same time people often lack the necessary understanding to make these decisions wisely. Thus people come to the church for help in finding their way through this perplexing world.

Often they seek not only spiritual and ethical guidance but also emotional and practical guidance. As a common example through the years, while persons might eventually set up an appointment with a psychologist, they frequently consult a pastor first. Similarly, while eventually parishioners will consult lawyers, they may first talk over the problems of their finances and wills with their ministers. In response to this increased reliance on the church for helping people through the maze of life, churches have set up their own counseling centers, legal assistance programs, financial advice seminars, and other educational endeavors that aid people's understanding.

On the other hand, people look for understandings from the church that will strengthen their hold on themselves. From every angle and at every moment of the day the world is hawking its wares. From body odor pitchmen to well-intended friends, people are bombarded with enticements of how they can become this or that, or are basted with guilt lest they not act thus or so. As a result, people are uncertain about their motives as well as their identities. While the church itself has contributed to this confusion at times by its own schismatic infighting, the church has stood remarkably firm in proclaiming the essential nature of people (they are God's children) and what is expected of them (to express and extend the love of God and the love of neighbor).[1] People look increasingly to the church for those solid understandings that can steady them as they face the vacillating winds of life.

3.

YEARNINGS TO BELONG IN THE CHURCH

A young man introduced himself to the pastor at the end of the service. "I'm a freshman at the college. This is my first real time away from home, so I'm feeling kind of lost. I haven't made any new friends at school yet. For some reason I just don't seem to fit in. I came today hoping to meet some people and to see if I could be a part of some group."

People come into the church longing to belong. They come with their normal needs to feel close to others. They come with their loneliness and with memories of never having felt included.

If people have been fortunate enough to enjoy supportive ties with others in the past, they look to the church for those normal, ongoing experiences of belonging that make life enjoyable and endurable. Furthermore, being securely connected to specific others, they are also able to identify with and affiliate with parishioners of diverse backgrounds and beliefs. When these people feel rebuffed in some way by those in the church, their self-esteem wavers, as does their general sense of well-being. This is a normal reaction when needs for belonging are thwarted. Emotionally strong people do not fall apart when this happens, however. They are still able to search for new relationships or to work out misunderstandings with others or to forgive those who have injured them. Likewise, their normal reactions of irritation and/or disappointment stay within appropriate limits. People who are basically assured that they are acceptable acknowledge that from time to time every congregation will fail to embrace them. That awareness, however, does not inhibit them from looking for unique companionship that is expected to be available in a community of faith.

People who suffer from chronic isolation, however, may come to the church looking for missed experiences of belonging, or for rectification of damaging relationships within other groups. Lacking the conviction of being acceptable, they may court the church's embrace of them. They may venerate the pastor and other parishioners as those quality figures with whom they long to be connected. Simultaneously, they may also demand that they be accepted by these idealized ones. However ostracized people may have been, they retain a cultural belief that the church cannot send them away. If people also lack firm identity, they may indiscriminately affiliate themselves with a specific religious community, shunning serious consideration of the appropriate fit between themselves and the particular congregation.

Lonely or rejected souls may also cling to curative fantasies about the church. These are fantasies of how one will be loved and made whole by being a part of a Christian community. At times these fantasies are sufficiently met to bring some restoration to the individuals. At other times individuals express grave despondency and anger at the church for failing to fulfill its embracing role.

Once again, there is a wide spectrum between these two poles in how parishioners use the church to meet needs for belonging. Perhaps no other image about the church has become so solidified in parishioners' minds as that of the church as a "people." And perhaps no motivation to join a church is stronger than a desire for a people with whom one can belong.

The search for a place to belong seems to be an especially pressing issue in contemporary life. In the midst of life's increased trivia, for instance, people long to feel they are part of others who are part of something important. People desire intimate connections not only to overcome normal loneliness, but also to feel linked with others whose ways and beliefs transcend culture's superficiality. Increasingly, people want to make a difference in the world. Consequently, they seek the company of those who try to embrace and care for the world, rather than try to dominate or dissect it.

Furthermore, there is a disenchantment with the "ticket of admission" into many groups. Gradually during the last two hundred years, and more rapidly in recent times, Western society has moved in an antiauthoritarian and democratizing direction. Liberalizing revolutions increasingly free persons from social, political, economic, racial, gender, and physical barriers. People expect at least a level playing field; that is, they expect a condition of equality in whatever place or job they enter. Unfortunately, true acceptance into certain groups is still based on race, sex, religion, financial status, academic degree, or health (few groups want an AIDS member, for instance). Even in more loosely organized groups, there is pressure to conform or "measure up."

People seek membership in groups that demonstrate both identity and quality. They have come to expect to be part of groups that uphold important values while making people, rather than people's functions or assets, of central importance. As individuals strive ever more urgently to find their own identity, they will look for membership in a group that will be supportive of their quest. In the church people hope to find a community they can proudly join, and into which they can feel warmly received.

4.

YEARNINGS FOR HOPE IN THE CHURCH

W hen our first daughter was born with brain damage, our minister came to be with us. He was a kind man. He stood with us quietly as we looked at our tube-riddled little baby through the intensive care window. I knew he was simply being with us in our agony. I knew he was giving us a chance to speak of our hurt. But that's not what we needed right then. With all our heart we wanted to hear something like, "You're all going to be okay. Things will work out fine. God will look after you." We yearned for a word of hope. We needed a hopeful vision of what might be so we could get through the long nights. We would not have held it against him if he were wrong. We merely looked to him for an encouraging word of hope that could sustain us until we were better able to endure reality and claim our own hope.

People come into the church seeking hope. They come yearning to place themselves in a hopeful environment that will enable them to face their yesterdays, todays, and tomorrows with confidence. They seek to be filled with that same hope themselves, so that they might be able to express to others and to God such words as these:

"For all that has been, we say amen."

"For all that is, we say thanks."

"For all that will be, we say yes!"

People who have been fortunate enough to grow up in a hope-inspiring environment look for the church to be a similar community of hope. They also rely on the church to sustain their buoyant spirits, especially when they are confronted with the raging storms of life that beat away at their visions and ideals. While they lean on the church as a source of hope, they also realistically acknowledge the church's limitations. When the church fails to be a sustainer of hope, these emotionally firm individuals are jolted but not fragmented. Their normal reactions of irritation and/or disappointment are expressed in ways that do no damage to themselves or others. They remain receptive to "good words" from pastors and lay members, and they search for a message in the difficulties that arise.

Other people come to the church with reduced hopes. In one way or another they have suffered blows to their cherished dreams. As a result of failing to reach these dreams, and in order to avoid the anxiety and despondency created by their loss, they retreat to more immediately obtainable goals. For example, a high school teacher who sadly acknowledges that her labors have not been responded to by those she is trying to help may devote more time to the solitary activity of lesson planning.

To the rest of the world the new goals may not seem to be reduced goals. The hope-injured individuals know differently, however. They know the move to "obtainable" goals is not simply a healthy adjustment but rather a self-protective measure. Although they miss the allurement of cherished dreams, they often feel too injured to mobilize their hope toward grand new goals.

Persons with reduced hopes may need to affiliate with a church dedicated to lofty projects. They may yearn to be part of a community that persists in its efforts no matter what the obstacles, whose vaulted aims remain clear and inspiring.

When the congregation appears to lose its dedication, or to settle for compromised goals, these particular parishioners may become scathing critics of the church. Their challenge that the congregation is "selling out" may be objectively true at times, but the intensity of the criticism stems also from the hurt they have suffered from the loss of their own special dreams.

Other individuals come into the church reluctant to hope. Perhaps they have been devastated by groping after false hopes. Perhaps they have always been fearful of "throwing their bread upon the water"—that is, they are fearful of making wrong choices in what to hope for or to hope in. These persons are often passive. Feeling uncertain of themselves, they try to avoid claiming major responsibility for decisions that affect them.

Such individuals may look for the church to give them assurances on which they can rely. They may seek promises and truths they can trust will not fail them. Hesitant to give direction to their own life, they depend on the guidance of the pastor and other parishioners. Such individuals do not claim their own hope and its energizing impulse to live responsibly. They lean, instead, on the ministrations of others for their sense of being marginally safe.

Finally, there are persons in every congregation who seem absent of hope. They either move through their days in a numb stupor, or they sit on the sideline criticizing those who are still plugging along in the race of life. Whether shell-shocked or embittered, it is hard for them to act hopeful or be receptive to encouragement. Quite often the pastor and other parishioners seriously wonder why these individuals come to church at all.

In many cases, such individuals secretly yearn for hope to be awakened in them. Their flat or combative behavior hides their desperate reliance on the minister or others for emotional salvation. Although often they cannot divulge it, the church may be their last hope for hope.

Our culture today is wish-riddled but not particularly hope-filled. Many people, for example, wish that they would win the lottery or that their astrological chart would come true or that something scary would magically go away. These individuals may wish for a better world, personally or globally, but are not filled with a hope that leads them to work for that better world. Stimulating hope in people's hearts is critically needed today, and it will be more so in the future.

People wish rather than hope when they feel futile. Goethe once observed that Hamlet's tragedy was that of "a great deed imposed upon a soul unequal to the performance of it."[1] In that same way today, people laboring in life with a burden of uncertainty and disappointment feel "unequal to the performance of it."

That sense of hopelessness is often passed on to the next generation. Many children live in families where hope is weak, or where there is a mood of accepted hopelessness. Mother and Father plod along, doing their duty, expecting tomorrow to be only a repeat of today's obligation. Drained of energy or lacking social support, the light dims in Mother's eyes, and Father's step is a resigned shuffle rather than a confident stride. Hope is not in the air for children to breathe freely and deeply.

As a result, the present moment for many children does not feel as if it is vibrantly alive. Their future does not energetically beckon to them with promise. They yearn for Mom and Dad to wake up with a happy smile as they begin their day. They long for their folks to be peppy and to plan things they can look forward to. Hope-lapsed parents generate a hope-limited world around their children, leaving them, in turn, to pass on the same depressed legacy.

In the next four chapters we explore how relationships within the church can be nurtured so that people feel understood, come to understand, know they belong, and find hope that sustains them all their days. We see, also, how a functional orientation in the church can threaten this ministry to persons.

5.

PREACHING THAT REACHES OUT

The scriptures tell us that the crowd around Jesus "heard him gladly." They did so because they found in Jesus one who reached out to them, who spoke the language of their hearts. People yearn for words of life from their preacher. Too often they are not gladdened by what they hear. While congregations can be notorious in their demands for how the pastor is to preach, preachers themselves often fail to adequately feed hungering souls.

Some ministers use preaching to "create an effect." The implicit purpose of their preaching is to generate sensations and feelings in parishioners. While this effort to stimulate people's emotions can be wholesome, we all have witnessed televangelists who manufacture experience as a substitute for genuine relating. The "effect" is primarily intended to lead to greater revenue or boosted ratings or more political clout.

While this functional, rather than truly relational, use of preaching may signal unethical behavior in some preachers, other ministers mistakenly believe that creating an effect on Sunday morning is, indeed, touching human hearts. The two are not synonymous, however. It is relatively easy to generate an artificial unity among strangers that quickly fades when the soaring music stops. Preaching to "make people feel good" (or to make them feel bad) is not necessarily preaching that builds an intimate fellowship. Effects lack real substance; they do not fill people up or strengthen them for an abundant life.

In this chapter we consider ways in which preaching can reach out to parishioners who yearn to feel understood, to understand, to know they belong, and to find hope. People will hear the preacher gladly, and will be blessed, when the words of faith are translated into the language of their hearts.

Conveying Understanding

A pastor told his congregation that he expected to be addressed as "Reverend" rather than by his first name because he had been set apart by God to deliver God's message to them. In his hands the sermon became an instrument for informing their minds and forming their behavior. The minister preached to his parishioners rather than reached out to them. While the congregation learned from that minister's head, they felt the painful absence of his understanding them with his heart.

People repair to the church hoping to feel connected with an understanding pastor. It is an appropriate yearning. It is equally appropriate for the pastor to preach in ways that fulfill this relational and spiritual need. Preaching conveys understanding when it is personal. Preaching also conveys understanding when the pastor radiates understanding through his or her person.

Preaching must resonate with personal needs. It must connect with the inner life of parishioners. It should convey a deep understanding of human pain and struggles, hopes and joys, everyday requirements and monotony, so that parishioners can say within themselves, "Someone has touched me. Someone has broken through my nobody-knows-me loneliness."

Good preachers know this. In seminary preaching classes we are instructed to "begin where the people are." It is stated aphoristically: "Before you can bring the Word to a starving person, you need to bring that person bread." Preaching, therefore, is grounded in experience; that is, it is rooted in the lived experiences of the congregation. Preaching is also relevant to experience—that is, it touches those emotions most crucial to people in their varied states of life.

A good shepherd knows the flock. Sermon preparation, consequently, begins by being with the people. The week before the Sunday sermon, the pastor would be advised to spend significant time sharing in the lives of the church family. That will mean interacting with people outside of church programs or committee work. It will mean such involvement as visiting the lonely in a nursing home, calling on a family that is going through rough times, or accepting an invitation to celebrate another's joy. One rural pastor spent part of each week working side by side with farmers in the congregation. At the top of the first page of sermon notes, the pastor can write the names of those people visited and prayed for during the week. The preacher can keep their faces and their fears in mind while studying the scriptural texts, for to them and similar others must the good news become powerfully alive.

Preaching directed at persons, however, means more than simply "incorporating" human experiences into the sermon or using understanding as a springboard for proclaiming the Word. The very aim of preaching is to convey understanding. *The essence of preaching is to convey to the children of God that they are understood.*

That was the purpose of Jesus' preaching. The word and act of his preaching sought to convey to the weak and heavy-laden that they were not alone but known, that God stood by them. His preaching was the embodiment of the Emmanuel message: A comforting, understanding presence surrounds you. Similarly for ministers, preaching should be that act by which the crowd around Jesus feels enveloped and understood.

Understanding is also conveyed through the person of the preacher. The yearning crowd around Jesus not only heard him gladly, but they also reached out to touch him and to be touched by him. Jesus not only expressed the life-giving, understanding word; Jesus embodied the life-giving, understanding word. The word of Jesus became incarnate in his person.

The same relationship happens with pastors. People who yearn for understanding reach out to touch the hem of the preacher's robe. By calling and by expectation, the preacher's *personal self* is made central in his or her ministry. Understanding is conveyed, therefore, not only by the pastor's words but also by the pastor's self. The preacher cannot hide behind preaching.

Pastors implicitly know this, but often they try to minimize the seminal importance of their personal selves in preaching. They have been supported in this disavowal by denominational teachings. In a variety of ways they have been taught that while in word and gesture they stand for the most hopeful message it is possible to convey to humankind, nonetheless the high dignity of their ministry derives not from them but from their message.

Theologically we know the important distinction being made here. But sooner or later we need to accept the fact that the "word and gesture" of the minister are inseparable from the whole self of the minister. A minister cannot have a full, incarnational preaching ministry by going off to the pulpit with just his or her "word and gesture" any more than a penis and vagina can go off to a cabin and have a full, meaningful relationship. Like it or not, in both cases a self is attached. Stated succinctly but with great affirmation, *the self of the pastor is central in preaching.*

Pastors complain, of course, even from the pulpit, about the dangers of ego, that one's own interests get in the way of God's work. "Not my will but yours be done" is the espoused goal. And rightly so. But the self of the pastor is always centrally involved. The *person* and the *role* of the preacher are inseparable. The pastor's self in preaching is a primary means of grace by which parishioners feel deeply understood.

The preacher's actions and attitudes in the pulpit, therefore, have the power to communicate understanding or to undercut intended words of understanding. The minister's stilted manner of gesturing or slightly grandiose way of sermonizing diminishes her or his image as one who warmly understands. If the pastor fails to look at the people when preaching, or looks uneasily at them, he or she depletes the comforting words of faith proclaimed. A preacher's tendency to complain from the pulpit or to talk too much about himself or herself or to be coolly detached and intellectual detracts from that pastor's being an empathic figure parishioners long to feel touched by and to touch. As the minister steps into the pulpit, his or her opening prayer can be "May the message from my whole being and the meditations of our hearts be acceptable to you, O Lord, our strength and our redeemer."

Helping Others Understand

People come to the church with a desire to understand. They look to the preacher for words of wisdom that will help them through confusing, crisis-laden times. They hunger for stability rooted in something eternal. They long to possess an understanding of what is real and permanent, and how they can follow that truth for their own contentment and salvation.

As one response to this yearning to understand, some preachers offer "prescriptive explanations"—attempts to help people understand what "is" and what "should be." The preacher proclaims how God has given us truths and laws to nurture us, how difficulties arise when people do not respond to God's intentions for us, and how we need to turn back to God in faithful obedience.

Jesus used prescriptive explanations in his preaching. Boldly he affirmed the former prescriptions for Israel: "Do not think that I have come to abolish the law or the prophets. . . . Whoever breaks one of the least of these commandments, and teaches others to do the same, will be called least in the kingdom of heaven" (Matt. 5:17-19).

Jesus, however, went beyond the law and prophets. "You have heard that it was said to those of ancient times," he proclaimed to the crowd around him as he quoted in turn the familiar mandates laid upon them. But in the next breath Jesus installed his own redefined moral prescriptions with the authoritative prelude, "But *I* say to you. . . . " Those prescriptions to the people were very specific and concrete, the most memorable being, "If anyone strikes you on the right cheek, turn the other also" (see Matt. 5:21-48).

Prescriptive explanations are commonly used by fundamentalist preachers, but are often avoided or watered down by other Protestant pastors. The reasons vary for why clergy eschew prescriptive explanations. Some may not affirm the Bible's reliability in moral discourse, or they may reject the notion that there are absolute ethical "truths." Other pastors may strive to avoid any impression of trying to manipulate others, or they may be reluctant to put themselves in a position of authority. But in the light of parishioners' need to understand, the avoidance of prescriptive explanations in preaching is an unfortunate over-reaction. Prescriptive explanations are both appropriate and necessary.

Prescriptive explanations are especially fortifying when a congregation or an individual feels vulnerable or is in a critical state of disintegration. At these times persons need strong guiding ideas and explanations to hold themselves together. In the midst of a crisis, a preacher's empathic but powerful statements that God is calling for humility, duty, or repentance can sustain individuals whose capacity to be led by their own understanding is temporarily diminished.

Prescriptive explanations, however, can become functionally oriented edicts. In this state they are used to hammer the "true and only way" into people. They rigidly focus on changing people's behavior rather than strengthening their understanding. A one-size-fits-all attitude prevails, with principles

applied universally and generally to all persons in all situations.
The result, on the one hand, is a lack of personal relevance.
Parishioners may desperately cling to the pastor's explanations because of their vulnerability, but without a feeling of being truly understood. On the other hand, such dogmatic explanations lack practicality. Concrete dictates on how to act fail to be relevant in the complexity of everyday life. One cannot, for example, simply live with the admonitions: "Wives, always be obedient to your husbands"; or "If you will just forgive, everything will work out fine"; or "We have no need for doctors, for God is our healer." Narrow-minded prescriptive explanations not only fail to convey compassion, but they also fail to nurture competent understanding.

Furthermore, rigid prescriptive explanations in preaching often alienate people, for they fail to provide tolerable forms of self-recognition. For example, great religious awakenings were apparently sparked while imagining oneself as a "sinner in the hands of an angry God," but this type of intense fire-and-brimstone preaching today does not generally lead parishioners to deepened self-awareness. Indeed, people are typically put off by such pronounced descriptions of their perilous condition. As an unfortunate result, the important message about our injuries to others, our ultimate accountability, and God's saving grace is lost to people who need to understand these realities. The prescriptive form is often made sacred in preaching when it is the message rather than the form that is the gospel.

Prescriptive explanations can be redeemed from their excesses by employing strategic abstractness. This means we preach in such a way that moral responsibilities are proclaimed to parishioners without dictating the moral details of their daily lives. Jesus often made his prescriptive explanations strategically abstract. Through parables and stories, he focused on the most concrete and important reality of all—namely, the need for people to respond to each other with thoughtful understanding. The stories were made graphic enough so that people could recognize that the moral applied to them, but the moral was directed to their head and heart rather than being applied as a new kind of pharisaic law. Jesus knew the damage that can occur when people rigidly concentrate on correctness.

A marvelous example of Jesus' use of strategic abstractness appears in his response to the Pharisees who were intent on tricking him into betraying God or betraying Caesar. They offered up a clever no-win proposition:

> "Teacher, we know that you are sincere, and teach the way of God in accordance with truth, and show deference to no one; for you do not regard people with partiality. Tell us, then, what you think. Is it lawful to pay taxes to the emperor, or not?"

And Jesus, looking straight through them and their deceit, rendered this stunning, strategically abstract moral injunction: " 'Give . . . to the emperor the things that are the emperor's, and to God the things that are God's' " (Matt. 22:15-22).

Strategic abstractness in our explanations focuses on principles and guidelines, on reminders of what is most important in human life, without dictating the particulars in every situation. Strategic abstractness at times helps us to avoid betraying the message and spirit Jesus gave us. It also helps preachers reclaim the legitimate use of prescriptive explanations in those situations where helping others understand is central to their emotional and spiritual salvation.

Freeing for Belonging

A functional orientation predominates when preaching is used to "bind" people to the church. This was quite literally the case with one pastor who deliberately preached forty-minute sermons "so that the membership will be in church at least one hour a week." Other clergy try to hold on to members by proclaiming that other churches are misguided if not sinful. Correlated with that are sermons intended to massage the egos of parishioners who, in contentment, then remain. Then again, there are sermons that intend to generate feelings of guilt in people lest they think of abandoning the work and needs of a particular parish.

People come into the church yearning to belong, not to be bound. Preaching at its best strives to *free* people for true belonging. While much could be said about overcoming social discriminations that keep persons from full acceptance within the church, our focus here is on how preaching can release parishioners from their own impediments to fellowship. When this happens, the church is ministering to persons, rather than persons functioning for the church.

Parishioners often need to be freed from the emotional constrictions that keep them from belonging. Guilt, for example, is a notorious saboteur of relationships. Guilt-ridden individuals feel unworthy of friendship, or else deem themselves such tremendous sinners that others could not possibly accept them. Grief, likewise, curtails belonging. Grief-ridden individuals claim that no others could ever fill the place of the lost loved ones, or else declare that they, too, have died inside. Anger also punctures opportunities for fellowship with others. Angry individuals snip away at innocent ones, or else turn away from others into self-pity. The minister confronts these intimacy-shunning reactions in preaching and, in the spirit of Jesus' beckoning love, seeks to liberate persons from them.

Such liberation may come as the preacher expresses from the pulpit understanding for what persons are going through. Empathic descriptions of the struggles people are having can begin to break down the barriers of their isolation. Such sensitive concern can help guarded parishioners feel, "Someone really does understand me. There are other people out there who have the same feelings I do." Furthermore, from the pulpit the preacher can lift up the truth of what individuals are sensing and thinking in their guilt, grief, or anger, for there *are* degrees of justification for their reactions. That also can begin to free persons from the hopelessness of ever being understood and accepted.

At the same time, the preacher may attempt to free individuals from the emotional excesses that keep them alienated from others. "Jesus got angry in his life," explained one minister. "He was angry at the Pharisees, he was angry at the moneychangers in the Temple, and he became irritated at the disciples. He understands our anger, too. But there is a difference between 'righteous indignation' and 'personal resentment.' The power of evil watches for every chance to turn our anger into something ugly. Watch that that doesn't happen with your anger." This prescriptive explanation did not attempt to suppress anger but rather to cast out the demonic perversions of anger that poison intimacy with others.

Preaching may also seek to free people from misguided conceptions that impede belonging. A parishioner once told of being severely hyperactive as a child. The medical condition itself did not cause him trauma, however, but the rejection he suffered because of it. Desperately in need of friendship he decided that he would "do" something to make himself popular, since who he "was" as a person apparently was not good enough. And so he became a grade-school track star, only to find that he was still pushed aside. When he entered high school, he clung to the new hope that his "thinking" would be his ticket for admission, since who he was and what he did brought no inclusion. And so he immersed himself in studies, became brainy and intellectual, only to endure the same alienation. In college he became so frightened of being rejected by the fraternities on campus that he took upon himself the mammoth task of creating a new fraternity, one made up of "misfits" who gravitated together. Later he joined a church, looking for the acceptance he never had, but assuming once again that who he was would not be sufficient for true belonging.

The liberating word he heard from the pulpit was that people are acceptable not because of what they do or what they think, but because of whose they are. "We are all God's children, and God loves us as we are," he heard proclaimed. "God teaches us to love each other unconditionally, as God in Christ loves us." That elemental but indispensable word loosened him from the misconceptions of what constituted belonging, and from the fear of rejection lest one not measure up. It released him to attempt again to fit in—not just with the congregation but with the whole human family.

That preaching also delivered him from the misconception that his belonging could only be with "misfits." The community into which he was invited was not presented as a gathering of the fringe of culture, but as a fellowship of those called by Christ. He heard the emancipating word we all need to hear: The Church is Christ's, and when Christ sits at table with his crowd, we are all made special. Preaching is intended to be a pastoral act of love, justice, and healing that seeks to free people for communion with each other and with their God.

Awakening Hope

Preaching is approached as a functional obligation by some pastors. It is part of the "job description" they know is required of them. To accomplish this task, such clergy may preach the published sermons of others, even though these sermons do not fit the hurts and pressing questions of the congregation. They may also "go through the motions" in the pulpit, reading the manuscript word for word, with little pastoral encouragement. Some ministers in this functional mode also preach without making any references to themselves at all. Personal testimonies or stories are avoided. While these sermons may be theologically correct, they are characteristically lifeless and without inspiring hope.

People turn to the church when they search for hope. They listen for words from the preacher that can renew the joyful expectancies they hold within. They long for an energizing word that can jump-start their deadened hearts. Preaching nurtures parishioners when it endeavors to awaken hope in them.

One particular way the pastor can inspire hope is by preaching with reverent imagination.[1] Hope is tied to imagination. Hope, on the one side, is imagining the future, of what is still possible. Hope in the present is also tied with imagination, for one must imagine that something meaningful is occurring in the moment. Furthermore, hope in the past is linked with imagination, for one must continually reinterpret one's story at each significant juncture of life.

What makes imagination reverent in preaching is that the pastor tries to be a faithful envisioner of how God has worked, is working, and will work for good in our lives. The pastor can rightly operate from the faith assumption that acts of reverent imagination (whether from the preacher or from parishioners) are not just human projections upon God, but are images of hope projected in us by God's very self. Reverent imagination can be "the kingdom of God within you."

Reverent imagination in preaching attempts to encourage hope by visualizing how God is engaged in our lives. The following sermon portion was intended to awaken parishioners from their numbness to God's working presence.

If you sit on the east side of the balcony on a Sunday morning when the bell is ringing, your whole body vibrates. I don't mean just a little. The church literally shakes up there with the strong swinging and clanging of the bell, and you shake along with it. Now you might ignore that event, or you might wonder if over the years the ringing of the bell will do structural damage to the church. But you might also begin to imagine something else. You might also wonder, "Is God calling me? Is God trying to move me, to shake me out of my complacency and empty routine? As I sit here vibrating, is God taking me by the shoulders and trying lovingly to get my attention?" Friends, this is not crazy thinking. Let your bodies be receptive to the working of God in every facet of your lives to make you more awake and more hopeful.

When you drive back from where you grew up, and if the memories there were painful and made you feel as if nothing was right—especially you—listen to the hum of your tires on the road. Listen to that sound and imagine in it the voice of the Holy Spirit whispering in your ear: "You were better than you thought you were, and you did more than you thought you did. You were better than you thought you were, and you did more than you thought you did." That is not craziness. It's being reverently open to God, who takes every occasion and sound to lift up your spirit.

When you return from the doctor's office and the report is ominously uncertain, and suddenly your tomorrows look short and black, shut your eyes and reach out and grab the hand that Jesus is stretching out to you. Hear him say, "It's you and me, dear one. I'm always going to be with you, no matter what happens, even when your body gives out and you feel low. Just squeeze my hand and know that I am here beside you." Let yourself imagine. That's one way God speaks to us and lets us know we are never alone.

Reverent imagination in preaching can be an act of encouragement that "sends a shining ray far down the future's broad'ning way," as an old hymn promises. Our future is not what it used to be when we know that God is ahead of us, waiting, loving. Reverent imagination in preaching can also be an encouragement that gives one hope and helps one cope in the bewildering present. Reverent imagination can likewise be an encouragement that allows parishioners to tell the stories of their past in new and more redeeming ways. Reverent imagination creates a hopeful world around us and in us.

Reverent imagination in sermons is not "Pollyannaish" or theatrical. It is an attempt to expose a vision of a new and brighter day, or a vision of deeper meaning in what has happened or is happening. We need not only to see a rainbow in all the storms that assault us, but to faithfully look for that rainbow as well.

Pastors can be inspired for this type of preaching by Jesus himself, whose reverent imagination still has the world gasping. The Sermon on the Mount, for example, continues to startle the imagination of the crowd with revelations of how God is working for glory in all that we consider grief. Reverent imagination in preaching can be both faithful and hope engendering. Ministers preach the good news when they are vision-givers and dream-keepers. Thus are people ministered to in ways that inspire them and please God.

6.

TEACHING THAT CONNECTS

The Sunday school teachers in my rural home church were not trained or religiously sophisticated. The materials they gave us to use often came from their own closets. The lessons they taught us developed week by week from dated teachers' manuals mixed with their own current experiences. But we children lacked for nothing, because those teachers possessed the most essential teaching skill of all: an intuitive sense that—while learning the Bible stories and how a Christian acts were important—most important was our feeling loved by God and by the congregation. Maybe that's why the old childhood song "Jesus Loves Me" always made me tingle. I knew something of Jesus' love for me because I sensed love from those teachers who loved Jesus.

A minister of Christian education in a well-heeled suburban church once remarked: "The most important part of my work is nurturing the teachers and students. I listen to teachers' stories and support them, and I try to help them help the children care for each other and to speak kindly to each other." She and my old Sunday school teachers would have gotten along just fine. They all knew that the purpose of teaching is to express and to extend the love of God and the love of neighbor. That should be the spirit that guides the heart and head of every teacher in the church, whether it be laity instructing students, a youth minister teaching confirmation, or a senior minister speaking to an adult study group.

Unfortunately, teachers in the church forget this. It gets lost when a functional orientation supplants the relational spirit in teaching. For example, teachers get caught up in the mechanics of teaching. One supervisor of Christian education said his most important task was "recruiting" teachers for the program and doing what he could to "resource" them (which meant making sure they had books, paper, crayons, and the like). A new-teachers' workshop, similarly, spent most of its Saturday morning time discussing how to use curriculum, how to integrate music into the classes, the importance of maintaining discipline, and how to contact parents when their children had not been in class for several consecutive Sundays. These "mechanics" are necessary, but often they become central. The devastating result is that children pick up on this. They implicitly sense that not they but the program is primary.

A functional orientation can also predominate in the espoused "goals" for teaching. Christian education, for instance, can be construed as moral training and preparation for membership in the church. Or adult education can be employed for the training of laity who have some functions they need to perform in the church. Then again, one pastor's rationale for proliferating a wide variety of classes was that "They are instruments for expanding lay involvement." While education for these purposes is valid, these functional purposes do not define the essence of Christian education. More important, they have the power to subvert the agenda of ministry to persons.

Teachers committed to nurturing relationships in the church will strive to connect intimately with those who come to learn. In what follows, we consider ways to establish that connectedness as we consider the four cardinal relational needs of people: to feel understood, to understand, to sense one belongs, and to find hope.

Creating an Understanding Environment

A functional orientation can operate as a hidden curriculum in teaching. For example, teaching within the church may be directed toward determining the life and faith of the learners. The ultimate focus becomes one of instilling biblical or religious knowledge, of inducing "Christian responses," of indoctrinating others so they will lose themselves for a great Christian cause, or of fortifying a particular theological position. Teaching in this framework begins with what the teachers expect the learners to do or to be and then proceeds toward achieving that end. The goal may be worthy, and the intent of teachers may be honorable, but the method basically bypasses the learner's personal life, needs, and perspective. As a result, not only does the teaching compromise its declared commitment to persons rather than to behavioral objectives, but it also proves to be ineffective. Teaching at its best begins with those who come to learn.

People come into the church yearning to feel understood. They strive for meaning during difficult times when they sense that their feelings are cared for and that others are truly concerned about whether they live or die. Feeling understood is not a "bonus" experience that some people enjoy as they develop and grow as persons. Feeling understood makes growth possible. Feeling understood is as indispensable for our emotional survival and personal development as oxygen is for our physical survival and bodily development. A person becomes a self by the grace of an understanding environment. *Who* a person becomes as a self is determined by the *quality* of that understanding environment.

Feeling understood is taken for granted by many of us. It simply exists silently in the background of our daily lives as mothers and fathers, relatives and friends, ministers and teachers responded thoughtfully to who we are and what we need. Then again, feeling understood may have been a "saving" experience for us, even a "conversion" experience, as the emptiness of our life was transformed by the nourishing words of a person we respected. Sensitive responses of an understanding teacher can transform young lives, while unempathic, authoritarian demands to "be who you are expected to be" can destroy young lives.

Learning, consequently, is not automatic. Teaching-learning only begins when the child, youth, or adult feels understood. Only when persons feel surrounded by a nurturing environment of understanding others can learning and growth become realities. That understanding spirit can be expressed when our Christian teaching attempts to connect with children, youth, and adults by creating an empathic environment around them. That understanding spirit can also be expressed when our Christian teaching creates specific empathic pathways between the teacher and the learner.

In order for learning to take place, our Christian education must begin by creating a *generally empathic atmosphere* for those who come to the church. As very obvious examples, effective church school teachers use material and language that fit with the cognitive maturity of their children, thus supporting children's need to feel proud of themselves and to have others feel proud of them. Likewise, understanding teachers use discipline in ways that protect the fragile selves of disruptive students while teaching them how to be kind. Empathic teachers of youth are attuned to the normal worries of young people about fitting in and being popular, consequently structuring learning situations that take these considerations into account. Successful teachers of adults are mindful of older people's wish to pass on their accumulated wisdom to others, and of the normal tendency of all of us to be protective of our own way of thinking and believing.

A generally empathic environment, however, is not simply a necessary preface to learning. An atmosphere that radiates understanding or that lacks understanding is itself a powerful teacher. When a teacher greets children with a cheery smile and affectionate touches, and when the teacher teaches with a joyful voice, then the children learn, through their hearts, that they are loved and that the church is a warm place to be. On the other hand, when the teacher greets children with formality or seems hassled or teaches with an authoritarian voice that keeps children in their place while the lesson is being imparted, then children learn, through their stomachs, that they are not particularly cherished and that the church is a wearisome place to be. Perhaps the most significant learning in the church comes not through the words one hears but through the vibrations one feels.

The whole church, however, is responsible for helping to create this nourishing empathic environment, not just the teachers. The quality of the congregation's interaction with children is very crucial. Children, for example, may merely be tolerated. They may not be spoken to as they move through the church halls. They may not be allowed in the worship service. There may be harsh restraints on them, like not running in church or being loud.

Youth often suffer the same rebuff. One church built a quarter of a million dollar youth center but refused to let the youth eat in it. Furthermore, that church's "youth" council was made up entirely of adults. When the young people of the church refused to come, the "youth" council blamed the youth director. Wisdom does not always prevail in places one would expect.

Teaching-learning takes place, however, not just with the establishment of a generally empathic environment. Teaching-learning proceeds only through the establishment of *pathways of empathy* with the learner's thoughts, feelings, and actions. This means more than saying that the learner will be resistant to learning new ideas or feeling new ways or acting differently until his or her thoughts, emotions, and behavior are acknowledged and validated. This is true, of course, but what we are saying here is that teaching-learning does not proceed until a connection has been made between the learner's existing thoughts and the newly offered thought, between the learner's present state of feelings and the newly described way of feeling, and between the learner's habitually relied upon ways of acting and the changed behavior suggested. A pathway must be established between what the learner experiences as "me" (one's lived experience) and what is as yet "not me" (the new thought, feeling, or behavior that is being offered for assimilation). The "not me" becomes "part of me" only as pathways of connections are made from the latter to the former.

Jesus was a master at doing this for the crowd around him. His parables always began by establishing empathic links to the lived experience of individuals. You know what it feels like to lose a sheep, don't you? You know the panic when you misplace your money, too. You know how dangerous it is out on the road and how robbers could jump you, beat you senseless, and take your possessions. You know how frustrating it is when you work hard to sow your seed and the birds eat it. And which one of you, having children, would give them stones to eat when they are hungry or snakes to play with? And then Jesus went on to connect those experiences with his new images for living the abundant life. Jesus seemed to know that unless some resonance was established with the lived thoughts, feelings, and actions of the person, the teaching would fall on infertile ground.

Similarly, the teacher must help to create pathways of empathy between the thoughts, feelings, and actions of the learner and the thoughts, feelings, and actions of Jesus in order for the Word to take root and grow. The Gospels become "the good news" as they touch something in the already existing life of the person's thoughts, feelings, and actions. Efforts to teach love for others or love for God, for example, must first attempt to establish empathic connections with the learner's prevailing history of loving and being loved. A pastor's attempt to teach a Christian meaning for human suffering must also make contact with the learner's own experiences with suffering, and with his or her various efforts to make sense of it. When Rabbi Harold Kushner wrote *When Bad Things Happen to Good People,* his very title made contact with the inner feelings of many readers, who *did* feel themselves to be basically good, who *did* feel themselves to be innocent victims. Similarly, the tremendous popularity of M. Scott Peck's teachings emanates from his ability to resonate with, and articulate, the struggles of many individuals. "Life is difficult," he begins in his book *The Road Less Traveled,* and voices seem to echo back, "He's right. Someone understands. Let's hear more." The point is that when empathic connections are made with a person's own experiences, then the person feels understood and becomes ready and capable of understanding.

This means, therefore, that teaching will involve a great deal of listening. The teacher will spend significant time listening to what the children want to say and to what they want the teacher to understand about their lives. This listening to the stories of others is not a waste. It is life-giving. In itself it reassures individuals that someone is genuinely interested in them. In addition, it gives the teacher a sense of how the learners are experiencing their lives so that the teacher can respond with even greater empathy in the teaching. Teaching that is relational rather than functional begins with those who yearn to feel understood.

Expanding Others' Understanding

Within the church it is commonplace to think that preaching is the hook that emotionally catches people, while teaching is a secondary activity that fills in the necessary content of who, what, why, and where. Not only is this an overly functional definition of teaching (and of preaching for that matter), but it is also erroneous. Teaching in itself is a transforming activity. Sitting in a confirmation class or a new members' study group may seem "safe," but it invites great adventure, if not risk. To open our minds consistently and deeply to the powerful messages of scripture and theology is to open ourselves to results greater than, and other than, those we anticipated.

People come into the church yearning for explanations that will illuminate the meaning of their lives. They make themselves receptive to explanations that will order their days and fortify their hold on who they are. They search for images and ideas that will beckon them toward new visions. When explanations lead parishioners to see the world differently, they inhabit a new world. They then have new understandings about themselves and their relationships with others, and about their relationship with God.

Such understanding and transformation do not always happen in a teaching-learning situation. The problem often lies in the approach taken to teaching and understanding. One approach is based on what we might call "the cult of self-validating expression." Teaching here is considered a process of *letting something come out* of a person. The teacher's goal is to "release" the wisdom or truth that is within a person and to "validate" the meaning that is inherent in the person's self-expression. Understanding, therefore, is defined as "being in touch" with oneself and one's vital urges. Understanding occurs when a person breaks through culture's imposed explanations and finds his or her own authentic meanings.

This approach is a remnant of the 1970s human potential movement, with its accent on self-actualization and "trusting your gut." It still operates within the church, especially with adolescent groups and in adult study groups where the expression of feelings rather than reflection on feelings is dominant. While this approach is certainly strong on empathizing with a person's experiences, by itself it does little to constructively carry forward experiences into new, mature perspectives. A person might feel understood but not really understand. All those good feelings from "being understood" cannot block the sensation that "something is yet missing." Children and youth as well as adults need to have their experiences honored, but they also need wise guides who can help initiate them into broader, more grounded understandings. The expression of feelings in and of itself is not understanding, nor does it necessarily bring transformation.

A second approach to teaching-learning is based on what we might call "the cult of great tradition." Here teaching is seen as the process of *putting something into* a person. Teaching is the imparting of a body of truths that is supposedly in the possession of those who teach it. Little or no attention is given to the experiences or questions that the learner brings to the situation. Understanding begins not with the stories of those who are to be taught, but with the rehearsal of the stories of the great tradition. Understanding, therefore, consists of having adequately assimilated the lessons.

This form of teaching is probably still dominant in our church school classes and adult study groups. While it correctly emphasizes the need to transmit religious truths, it often lacks empathic regard for the learner's experiences. As a result, a parishioner may "understand" with his or her head but not feel understood. More than this, a parishioner may suffer from explanatory indigestion. The lessons taken in remain as semi-foreign food. They are now "in me" but not "of me." The teaching of great tradition assumes that the material will become a part of the learner's self—sooner or later. When we face the reality of persons who have mastered the lessons but whose lives are still a mess, we must question the working assumption of this approach.

Teaching can bring understanding and transformation, however, as it stays empathically connected to people. In the last section we discussed how teaching should attempt to create an "empathic environment" in which learning can take place. We then said that teaching-learning proceeds as the learner feels understood, as "pathways of empathy" are created between the lived experience of the learner and the message given. But this does not complete the process.

A person understands—that is, comes to a new, altered state of perceiving and being—when *perspective explanations* "carry forward" the person's lived experiences. Note that the phrase here is "perspective explanations," not "prescriptive explanations." The story of a person's life is changed as he or she comes to see the meaning of that story from a new perspective.

Understanding occurs, therefore, when two basic events happen: (1) the person feels understood by others (his or her life experiences are taken seriously and an effort is made to connect the teaching to those experiences) and (2) the experiences of the person are carried forward into new realms of meaning and significance by the new perspective explanations offered to the person.

For example, a woman in her early thirties joined a church for the first time. She was filled with self-doubts. She worried, for example, that she wasn't a good enough mother and that she didn't believe strongly enough in God. She started to attend a study group in the church, whose members listened to her expressions of anguish and affirmed having similar worries as hers. For the first time she felt understood. That in itself was a new learning experience, along with the new awareness that she was not alone in being plagued by doubts.

But she was given more. As she and the group shared the burden of not feeling good enough, the leader suggested a new perspective. "Jesus came to tell us that God is a loving God rather than a vengeful God. God tenderly *watches over us* rather than sternly *watches us* for signs of disbelief or disobedience. Perhaps God agonizes with us when we agonize and takes our worries as signs of just how much we are really trying."

The woman found herself blessed with a new understanding. Her experiences, once couched in negative meanings, were now carried forward into a realm of new, hopeful meanings. She was now in possession of a perspective explanation that could support her when the old ruminations tried to whisper how bad she was. Teaching had provided an explanation that was not only empathic to her condition but that also broadened her perspective on the fuller meaning of her struggles. Children, youth, and adults come to new understandings by means of faithfully grounded perspective explanations that are empathically attuned to their experiences, thus allowing their experiences to be carried forward into new realms of meaning and value.

Teachers will thoughtfully experiment with various perspective explanations. Not all explanations will resonate with the child, youth, or adult's experiences, nor carry them forward. There are a variety of ways to convey the message of Jesus to the crowd who yearns for new understandings. A teacher who gets stuck in teaching the same content the same way year after year, as if the learners were all the same, will probably fail to connect adequately with those who come. A one-size-fits-all mentality is not an empathic mentality. Such teachers do not have years of teaching experience; they tend to have one year of teaching experience repeated many times. And that one year may not have been all that great. The hard, but rewarding, work of teaching is trying to translate the life-giving words of Jesus in ways that touch people's inner lives and carry them forward into the light of new understanding. Those clergy and lay leaders committed to the nurturing of relationships in the church will take this "road less traveled."

Supporting Belonging

One of the reasons adults give most frequently for joining a study group in the church is to feel that they belong. Apart from parental expectations, probably the most compelling personal reason young people come to confirmation or Sunday morning class is to be with their friends. Feeling we belong is not a luxury of life. It is a necessity for living fully. Belonging creates within us the basic assurance of being human and of being connected with humanity. This longing to belong is often the central yearning of parishioners—young and old.

Some teachers allow themselves and their teaching to be used for this purpose of belonging. I once led a seminar on parenting for members of our church. Before the first session, several individuals contacted me and said that they were not parents, but that they were new to the church and wanted to come so they might get to know some people. I assured them that they were most welcome. In doing so I was letting them "use" the situation for their primary need. They were not coming principally to learn; they were not there to hear what I had to teach them. They were there for companionship, for sensing that they belonged and were accepted. Fortunately at that time, I did not need them to be there for *my* agenda, nor to make me feel good about myself through my teaching. Teaching that is relationally oriented allows itself to be "used" by people with pressing needs other than the specific need to learn. Stated another way, teaching directs itself to the whole of persons rather than just to parts of persons.

Some teachers, however, have difficulty letting themselves be used in healthy ways. If they sense, for example, that young people are gathering in a class more to be together than to learn from the teacher, then these teachers tend to feel resentful if not outraged. Similarly, when some individuals show up repeatedly for various adult seminars the minister conducts, and the minister begins to realize that these individuals are widows, widowers, and single lonely people who come basically for companionship rather than to expand their understanding, the minister may then feel unappreciated and may lose enthusiasm for teaching.

The difficulty becomes more pronounced when teachers expect their classes to function *for them*. In this situation, teaching becomes a means by which teachers seek to gain personal satisfaction or to assure themselves that they are competent or to enhance their own self-esteem. When classes (and the people in them) do not function in ways that meet the teachers' expectations, the teachers tend to respond with mixtures of despair and anger. More specifically, when people come to classes to socialize, overcome loneliness, or find a kindred soul, this feels like a slap in the face to the teachers, who need *their* teaching to be the central motivation and interest of those who come. If a spirit of belonging occurs as a *result* of their teaching, or if a sense of belonging *prepares* people for learning or *enhances* the learning, then the need to belong can be accepted. But if the need to belong seems to be the primary, even equal, motive for coming, teachers can feel insulted and minimized.

Confident teachers committed to a ministry to whole persons, however, will support the use of the teaching situation as a way of meeting people's primary need to feel that they belong. Consequently, they will strive to tolerate patiently the presence of people who seem simply "there." Sunday school teachers must often deal with disruptive children who constantly talk when they should be listening, who get into things when they should be doing a project, and who sometimes run around wildly. While these children's disruptive behavior must not be allowed, the children themselves must be accepted. Children, like adults, are most in need of knowing they are accepted and belong when they are most unlikable and unwanted.

Likewise, teachers of youth often meet apparently snobbish visitors who come with youth group members. The rudeness of the visitor may be a genuine sign of contempt, but it may also be a way of not letting oneself be hurt. In any regard, the teacher attempts to extend a warm welcome and encourages the regular group members to respond to the visitor with friendship. Realizing that one is accepted in spite of oneself is a saving experience for many people, young and old. In the assurance that one is received and included, lives become transformed.

A person's sense of belonging comes not only from having received from others. It also comes from having given to others. A congregation's receptivity to what a parishioner has to offer is telling evidence for that parishioner as to whether she or he truly belongs.

Teaching can strengthen parishioners' assurance of being heartily included. Teachers do this by being receptive to what the learner has to give in the teaching-learning situation. This can come about in two ways.

One way is by the traditional means of soliciting people's help. Church school teachers strengthen belonging not just by urging children to participate but by having children help. Distributing pencils and paper, pouring juice, helping each other find Bible verses—all these "giving" rather than "required" acts contribute to warm feelings of being special and needed. Similarly, young people in confirmation experience a greater sense of ownership of the class and a deeper affection for each other when they have a hand in structuring their time together. Belonging is affirmed when big and small parishioners are invited to give their help in the procedures of the teaching situation.

The second way to strengthen belonging is for teachers to make teaching-learning an act of mutual give and take. Here the learner's comments are not just elicited; he or she is not just listened to perfunctorily or courteously. The learner's offered comments are genuinely appreciated—and needed. What the parishioner has to give is received as necessary for *everyone's* learning, including the formally appointed teacher. The "student" is also acknowledged as a "teacher," whose questions, insights, agreements, or doubts are taken as indispensable to the learning of all. Teaching-learning is here lived out as a community affair. The teacher realizes, therefore, that she or he cannot take sole credit for what is learned. It is a gift to the teacher from others (students included), and through the teacher to others. Each person's experiences are carried forward in some way by the responses of everyone else.

Related to this assurance of belonging through mutual give and take in teaching is the tremendous solidification of belonging that occurs when a parishioner participates in a shared construction of meaning. When a person carries within himself or herself the great satisfaction of having found and created meaning with others, indelible ties are made with those others. We see this happen with youth groups on retreats, when individuals experience the exhilaration of intimate "we-ness" as everyone's feelings and thoughts are embraced by everyone else, leading to a new understanding of, and feeling for, the group.

This happens with theologically sophisticated adults as well. A denominationally supported symposium resulted in the group writing of a consentual "affirmation of evangelism." This experience of constructing shared meanings gave rise to jubilant feelings of camaraderie. "This affirmation and our consensus are high points in my life in the church," they tend to say. "This was more than a meeting. It was an experience of the Holy Spirit in us." These lay and clergy leaders were like the retreaters—caught up in the exhilaration of being a created community as they joined together in the creation of meaning.

Teaching is not just for learning. Teaching is also for conveying to people that they belong. A church's ministry to persons embraces the whole of persons, leading it to rejoice when persons experience in some way the love of Jesus and the love of the crowd around him.

Instructing for Hope

One sign of a functional orientation within a congregation is the assumption that importing instructional techniques from the secular world will heal educational problems within the church. There is no doubt that learning from the science of teaching can greatly benefit the effectiveness of Sunday school teachers. But the essence of Christian education is something other than the function of teaching. Christian education has to do with knowing who we are as a community—namely, a crowd around Jesus—and knowing how to express

and expand the love of God and the love of neighbor. We lose
our identity, or at least compromise it, when we get too caught
up in successful performance.

But we need not reject instructional techniques. Just as we
sought to redeem prescriptive explanations for the purpose of
restoring relationships, so, too, can we seek to redeem instructional techniques. One means by which instructional techniques can nurture people and their relationships within the
church is by instructing for hope.

People in the church yearn for hope. They seek uplifting
assurance for what has been. They look for pastors and teachers who will paint smiling suns in their presently gray skies.
They listen for sounds of new promise.

Very frequently, however, people learn to feel helpless and
hopeless.[1] When a stressful situation occurs, it is natural for
individuals to have an initial reaction of anxiety and self-
doubt. But if individuals come to believe that control over
their stressful situation is beyond them, or that their efforts are
inadequate, then their initial anxiety and self-doubt may be
replaced with a sense of helplessness. Eventually, a response
of helplessness becomes the learned response to each new
occasion of stress, without the individuals' even testing
whether they can reduce their suffering or increase their grati-
fication in that particular situation. Motivation, consequently,
sinks to zero, and individuals disown any significant control
over their own lives.

While only certain parishioners exhibit chronic cases of
"learned helplessness," all of us at times become paralyzed by
traumatic events. Our hope plummets, and we doubt whether
we have any ability to change things. We become fearful of
making mistakes, and we try to avoid responsibility for decisions that affect us.

Teaching within the church becomes an act of encouragement
when it helps people reclaim hope. One way teachers can do this
is by fostering "learned hopefulness." Christian teaching can
encourage learners to respond to each occasion of stress with

appropriately hopeful statements, rather than with hopeless disclaimers. The consistent practice of meeting difficult times with hopeful statements of faith can generate a mood of expectancy that uplifts parishioners and moves them to try again.

This process of helping parishioners reclaim hope through learned hopefulness tends to happen indirectly in Christian education. Bible studies, for example, may focus on the hapless spirit of the people of Israel, who met each adversity in the wilderness with hopeless complaints, until eventually they learned that God was not only shielding them but had purposes for them. Parishioners may study the learned helplessness expressed by despondent psalmists, who, when the stressful occasion was resolved, declared how they had come to see the wisdom of holding on to hope at all times since God was never absent from them, even in their most hellish moments. Then again, parishioners may be instructed by the example of Jesus in the Garden of Gethsemane. He was sorely tempted to resign all hope, but instead faced his death and made it his own. Book studies and film reviews as part of the teaching ministry of the church may likewise lift up the heroic efforts of women and men to overcome adversity, thus subtly helping parishioners learn hopefulness.

Teaching, however, can make this process of learned hopefulness a more conscious agenda. The learning by inspiring example can be augmented with learning by explicit direction. Here learners are (1) taught the foundations of Christian hope, (2) given explicit faith statements that express this hope, and (3) instructed to pair each event in life, especially the stressful ones, with these Christian hope statements.

The following is an example of a way to teach learned hopefulness by directly linking an expanded understanding of God as the source of our hope with the whole sweep of our life story.

In the Bible, hope is not primarily a subjective experience but an objective reality—namely, the reality of what God has done and has promised. God is the source of hope, its sustaining power, and its certain object. To have hope, therefore, means to believe and trust in the promises of God.

We can see the implications of this for us in the Old Testament book of Exodus, in chapter 3, where God reveals God's name to Moses. God says to Moses, "Say this to the people of Israel, 'I AM has sent me to you.' " Now that's a very mysterious name, I AM. Perhaps we can understand a bit of this name's meaning when we read in the first chapter of the New Testament book of Revelations these words: " '*I am* the Alpha and the Omega,' says the Lord God, who is and who was and who is to come" (Rev. 1:8, emphasis added).

God seems to be saying to you and me, "I *was* with you and I *am* with you and I *will be* with you because *that's who I am.*" God, the great I AM, is that powerful presence who has always been circling through and in our past, who is daily providing the glue that holds us together, and who is waiting ahead of us to comfort and guide us. That's God's promise. That's God's *nature.* God is with us in our story, from its beginning, through its middle, and at its end, because, as God says, "That's who I AM."

We need to remember that, especially when times get rough for us. When we feel like the stuffing is being knocked out of us, and we begin to doubt whether we can get up and continue on, let us repeat to ourselves these words from God: "I was with you and I am with you and I will be with you because that's who I am." Let the cadence of those words give a beat to our step, and the power of those words give strength to our doing.

Conscious thoughts about hope in God will be taught over and over. Furthermore, the statements that express that hope will be varied. But the teaching can be clearly focused, by explicitly and consistently encouraging people to reclaim hope by meeting each stressful event in life with the hope-filled words of our Christian faith.

7.

CHURCH ADMINISTRATION THAT CARES

The typically acknowledged agenda of a church council is to do the business of the church—and rightly so. "Doing the business" may be accomplished not only with skill but also with a sense of service to others and to God.

That is not always the case, however. The debilitating presence of a functional mentality too easily emerges. One indication of this is when church councils get caught up in overmanaging. For example, people on the council, staff, and various church committees may be assigned definitive roles with clearly defined lines of responsibility and reporting. Even if a group springs up spontaneously from a circle of parishioners in response to a particular need, it may be expected to place itself under the supervising umbrella of some established committee. As another example, one clergy with a corporation management orientation suggested that various committees of the church council establish their own "advocacy groups" in order to lobby for their own programs. Similarly, church councils functionally overmanage, and treat parishioners as patrons, when they decide not to tell parishioners the budgetary needs of the church for the next year, lest parishioners only increase their giving to meet the budget, rather than give what they ought to give. As we said in our introduction, the church can dissipate into functioning for its own functioning. Clergy and lay leaders committed to nurturing people and relationships within the church must work toward making the church council a caring group.

Acting and Programming with Understanding

Church councils can regain their call to be ministers to persons by incorporating the awareness that people yearn to feel understood. One way they can do that is for council members themselves to act with understanding toward each other. Another way is to come to the programming aspects of their work with understanding for parishioners.

There's a secret about clergy that their families know all too well. When a minister comes home from the outside world, he or she often leaves understanding on the doorstep. Families of clergy commonly long for the same energy, patience, and compassion that the minister has given all day to others.

In the same way, council members and the pastor often leave their capacities for understanding and caring at the doorstep of the council room. They may do this because they assume that this gathering is not for the purpose of personal sharing or mutual support but for the conducting of administrative business. Or they may act cordially to each other (most of the time) but not interact with intentional concern because they consider the council meeting to be a forum for expressing opinions and frustrations.

But council members and the pastor come into the council room with their own yearnings to feel understood. Whether acknowledged, disavowed, or deemed inappropriate, council and clergy look for understanding responses from all present. That is typically the unspoken agenda operating beneath the official agenda of "doing the business" of the church. Indeed, much of the conflict and unproductive work that exists in church councils is rooted in the emotional injuries individuals feel they have suffered in those meetings. It is hard enough to endure the blow to one's self-esteem when one's championed idea is voted down. When that championed idea is treated with flippancy or disdain, the injury to oneself is even more devastating. Council members and pastor alike come to the work of the church hoping to be treated with respect and understanding.

A focus on getting things done can do more than fail to be understanding of people; it can also degrade people. For example, a man who was relatively new to a church and to membership on the church council stood up at his first annual meeting and moved that five thousand dollars of mission money be given to starving persons in Africa. The motion was approved. Later that day he was verbally thrashed by the senior pastor, who claimed that the council member had been disloyal to him by not checking out such an idea with him first. The council member's defense that he thought such a motion was constitutionally appropriate was met with the pastor's reply, "That's not how things of that magnitude are done here."

On the other side, a new minister was soundly rebuffed by the church council when he tried to change the custom of letting any couple be married in the church by any pastor of their choice. He was soon set straight that this was *their* church, not his.

Council members and clergy are often fearful of saying what they really think because they're uncertain of each other. Without feeling secure that they know each other as persons, and without the security of knowing that the expression and extension of the love of God and the love of neighbor is an enacted value in the group, they come to believe that their opinions may get them into trouble. As a result, they quickly learn their place and play by the rules. Smooth administrative functioning then occurs as a result of intimidation and acquiescence to intimidation, rather than from internal harmony and mutual support.

Church council members need to act with understanding toward each other. Some part of each session, for example, would best be spent catching up on how everyone is, praying for one another, praying for understanding, or supporting a distressed member.

A particular situation in which understanding might be practiced is when a female council member wants to talk about how she finds gender issues present in the administration of the church. To be able to name her experiences as a woman, to be given the time to tell how it feels to be a female in the administrative work of the council, to be empathically received as she tells of the kinds of biases that trivialize her efforts—all these are exceedingly important to her as a person. They are also vital for the soul of the council.

This type of sharing is not something for "outside" the council meeting, or something that should be reserved for a social retreat time. Encouraging expression of feelings and listening with understanding are at the heart of the council, even when the content is business. The council meeting does not then become group therapy. It becomes what at its core it should be: an extension of Jesus' care for all persons at all times in all places.

Pastors, likewise, need the council's understanding. Pastors have few, if any, groups in the church by whom they feel personally and professionally supported. Ministers may be required to "drive the business along" in council meetings, or they may feel the need to remain pastoral at all times, including council sessions. But council gatherings afford parishioners the opportunity to reach out to pastors who yearn to be understood as persons with feelings, not just as leaders with duties.

The council also benefits from being able to laugh together. While several members might joke among themselves before the council meetings, some appropriate light story or amusing anecdote shared with the convened group can help the members feel human and drawn together. It is especially helpful for the council to laugh at themselves. Laughing at themselves keeps the council members from taking themselves too seriously. Lifting up the foibles of the group from time to time can help the council realize their limitations while holding on to their self-esteem.

The church's council work is enhanced not only by acting with understanding toward each other but also by programming with understanding. This means, on the one hand, considering every piece of church business and every decision made in the light of their impact on the lives of parishioners. Each discussion over a new chair lift, the use of inclusive language in worship, the quality of toilet paper to buy, or the opening of the building to outside groups should be immersed in thoughtful consideration of the impact on individual souls. Each expenditure of money, each policy statement made, is attached to the heart of a person whose sense of life's fairness and love's presence is affected in some way.

The most flagrant "sin" of church councils occurs in their bypassing efforts to understand their programming decisions. Their most frequent failing is giving only cursory consideration to the impact of their decisions. The most beguiling error of church councils is operating from a self-referent stance.

A six-foot-seven-inch church member installed a new urinal in the men's remodeled washroom. Unfortunately, he adjusted the urinal's height to what seemed natural to him, leaving the bulk of mankind on tiptoes. Church councils, like other groups, often operate from a similar mentality of "what seems right to us." While they appear to be open to new understandings, they hold tightly to preformed ideas about what they deem necessary and needed by the church. As a result, churches often establish programs and then try to recruit people to fit in. People are molded to the program rather than the program's being fitted to the people. Moreover, church councils and/or clergy can appear so unapproachable and set in their ways that people give up trying to express alternative needs, with the result that, in the absence of contrary opinions, the council and/or clergy consider their views validated.

Understanding others is difficult enough for a single individual, such as the minister, but church councils must also try. In their own way, they must try to observe the life of parishioners, reflect on what they think they see there, and then reimmerse themselves with the people to test what they thought they had come to understand.

An understanding of parishioners and parish life does not tell council members what specifically to do. Such an understanding does give the minister and the church council a clearer perspective for creating or revising programs that maximize understanding within the congregation, however. With some practice and guidance, the understandings can be utilized in saving ways.

Finally, it is possible to visualize the *total* thrust of the church council's efforts as the maximizing of understanding within the congregation. Maximizing understanding can become central to the church's affirmed identity. The church council, therefore, can make central to its calling the conscious, deliberate effort to work toward a wiser, more understanding state of being—within itself and within the total community.

Anchoring and Opening Others' Understanding

The crowd around Jesus looks to understand itself as a group. A state of well-being is enhanced in parishioners when, as a congregation, they know who they are and where they are going. Congregations who lose touch with their history have difficulty marching securely into the future. Congregations who lose visions of their future have difficulty tapping into the support their history holds. Church councils have a responsibility for contributing to parishioners' understanding. They do this when they preserve cornerstone explanations. They also do this when they open themselves and their congregations to transforming explanations.

When a church becomes functionally oriented, however, the church's past and its traditions tend to be used decoratively, promotionally, or coercively. Traditions are paraded out for reasons other than anchoring the understanding and sustaining the spirit of the congregation. For example, a church who mostly ignored its past touted its history in front of the town during the latter's bicentennial. Another church lifted up its historical affiliation with its denomination when that denomination began to enjoy positive notoriety in the national press. Another church defended its practice of maintaining an ethnic membership by appealing to the church's origins and beginnings.

Furthermore, when a functional orientation prevails, explanations do not open people to understanding the future as the occasion for God's transforming work. Instead, the future is discussed in terms of "facing necessary changes," or of "keeping abreast of the times," or of "making adjustments." Church councils contribute to parishioners' understanding and to the building up of supportive relationships when they preserve cornerstone explanations and offer transforming explanations.

For example, a new pastor came to his first church council meeting with a definite purpose in mind. First he wanted to know from them what kind of church this was. "What have been St. J's strengths over the years? How has it served? What role has it had in the community and the denomination?" Next he asked the council what thoughts they had about where the church was going. "What work yet needs to be done? What potentials do we have? Where do you think the Spirit is leading us?" While he had read the dossier of the church before accepting the position, he was attempting to orient himself to the church, and to orient the church to himself.

But half-consciously he was doing more. Here at the beginning he was urging the council to rehearse the church's history and to verify those cornerstone strengths that made it what it was. At the same time, he was nudging the council to play with new images for the church, to envision a transformed future.

One step beyond this would have been to suggest to the church council that part of its explicit role would be to nurture the congregation's understanding of itself by (1) preserving the congregation's heritage and (2) ushering in new visions for the congregation's future.

Cornerstone explanations are those distilled statements of faith, work, personality, and attitude that have given a community its particular self-identity over time. The community of Israel confirms its cornerstone explanations from generation to generation, beginning with the familiar Passover words: "A wandering Aramean was my ancestor" (Deut. 26:5). The Christian community's first full cornerstone explanation of its identity emerged with the Nicene Creed:

> We believe in one God,
> the Father, the Almighty,
> maker of heaven and earth,
> of all that is, seen and unseen.

Similarly, each congregation has a story that lifts up those essential creation energies and core traits that imprint it with uniqueness.

A task for the church council is to consolidate self-understanding within a congregation by preserving its unique story. The council need not consider itself the bearer or representative of the church's tradition, but rather the preserver of that tradition. A council does this when it helps implement an annual "Heritage Sunday" that explicitly celebrates the founding of the church and the Spirit of God working through it. Parishioners' self-understanding is fostered also with updated publications of the church's history, with a small permanent display of important archival objects, and with a requirement that confirmands and new adult members be exposed to an interpretation of the congregation's historic traditions and standards.

Preserving cornerstone explanations also entails guarding them. The council attempts to protect its precious history against the onslaught of disgruntled parishioners and external critics. Tradition bashing is an old method used in attempts to get even with the church or to destroy it. On the other hand, tradition veneration can itself be nothing more than a resistance against new self-understandings. At its best, tradition gives continuity and cohesion to the congregation. Alzheimer's patients in the early stages of that disease lose a sense of being whole persons when they cannot remember who they were and what they did. Congregations suffer similar fragmentation of self when they lose the narrative line of their story.

Congregations are also in need of transforming explanations. As the old hymn reminds us, "New occasions teach new duties, time makes ancient good uncouth." A congregation must constantly redefine itself. New occasions call for new responses from the congregation, and thus for new awareness of who it is and is becoming. Congregations are particularly in need of transforming explanations when narrow values and habitual ways of responding leave them stagnant.

Church councils minister to parishioners' understanding when they make transforming explanations available. That means the council and pastor will work diligently to assess the congregation's needs and to open the congregation to new changes prompted by the leading of God's Spirit. It may mean inviting in a consultant who is capable of empathically understanding the congregation and empathically offering insights into its personality. It may mean bringing in a denominational staff member who can reflect anew on the theological meaning of the church's present condition. Then again, transforming explanations may come from a pastoral psychologist who offers new interpretations and new language to an immobilized congregation.

Councils are better at preserving cornerstone explanations than at initiating transforming explanations. An interim pastor once wrote to me, asking how to motivate her congregation into taking a serious look at itself. Denominational officials report the reluctance of church councils to call them for help when problems arise. Those who provide consultation to churches tell of the difficulty of getting churches to make significant changes in how they function and see themselves. Church councils (and ministers) are poor at making assessments of the church and its future, and at seeking outside assistance to help with this. Lack of time, expertise, or funds may partially account for this failure. Excessive pride, shame over difficulties, and fear of conflict, however, are the major reasons church councils avoid opportunities for an in-depth appraisal of the congregation's future.

As a result, the understanding necessary for dealing with tomorrow is denied congregations. Anxious parishioners may then hold on even tighter to the "old ways," for there are no secure transforming explanations showing the people what they can become. Other parishioners may simply rig their parachutes and jump from the pilotless church rather than learn to fly it.

The crowd around Jesus maintains cohesion as cornerstone and transforming explanations strengthen communal understanding. Parishioners can then lean on the memory of who they have been while leaning toward the self they can possibly become.

Maintaining Boundaries for Belonging

Parishioners' sense of secure belonging is rooted in part in an assurance that their community has definition and permanency. When a congregation maintains a consistent identity over time, parishioners feel connected to something enduring. Both pride in belonging and confidence in continued belonging are engendered when the community exhibits particularity and longevity.

Simultaneously, parishioners look to belong to a community that is embracing and compassionate. When a congregation conducts itself in wise and loving ways toward all people, parishioners feel connected to something larger than themselves, to something of quality that represents God in the world. Again, pride in belonging and commitment to belonging are enhanced when the community exhibits openness and care for all of God's people.

A church council responds to parishioners' yearnings for an enduring and embracing fellowship by maintaining healthy community boundaries. More specifically, a church council nurtures relationships and a sense of belonging by maintaining communal boundaries that are neither too particular nor too wide.

Consider the letter *w* in the word *we*. If the arms of the *w* are turned inward so that they nearly touch, the community of "we" is too narrow. It will have particularity, but it will tend to be exclusive of those "not like us." On the other hand, if the arms of the *w* are turned outward and downward in exaggerated openness, the community loses its identifying shape. When that happens, a "we" community has become too inclusive. Church councils are faced with the dual task of building bridges while also establishing borders. That's not easy to do.

The task is made more difficult when a functional orientation in a congregation begins to dictate boundaries and determine who belongs. Churches can be subtly to overtly exclusive, on the one hand. One church considered itself made up of self-starters, who were energized for tasks and dedicated to following through. They were not receptive to members who seemed less goal oriented than they. Another church organized itself on the basis of certain ethnic principles and attitudes. Their effort to maintain their "way of doing things" made it difficult for ethnically different families to join.

Churches can become overly inclusive, on the other hand. A desire to expand in size, or the necessity to increase numbers to ensure survival, can result in churches eliminating "marks of membership." Congregations thereby become all things to all people, equating expansion with growth and substituting cleverness for real communication.

Church councils need to watch lest their communities become too foreclosed or too diffused. When this happens, the needs of people to belong to enduring and embracing congregations are thwarted. Consequently, church councils can stay focused on establishing healthy boundaries. They can, for instance, be guided by the awareness that, while ethnic or communal exclusiveness creates fierce loyalty among church members, it deprives parishioners of the opportunity for broader based fellowship. Enclosed churches react to "invaders" by either rejecting them or ingesting them. With their clubby consensus of like minds, they fail to be blessed by including the differences and the unlikeness within the human family. The foreclosing on belonging privatizes the kingdom of God, and thus is an affront to humankind and to the Creator.

In addition, the church council can be guided by the realization that when a congregation suffers the erosion of its particularity (or more accurately put, when a congregation's religious traditions and faith are dissolved and united with anything) the community then loses its identity and power. Worshiping a "God-in-general" is not worshiping "the God and Father of our Lord Jesus Christ." Similarly, a "community-in-general," where all thoughts and doctrines are embraced, is not the community of Christ. In a community-in-general under a God-in-general all things are possible—which means the community stands for nothing except plurality.

Overly inclusive churches ultimately fail to be something to be a part of. Lacking integrity and definition, they offer little substance to sustain belonging. When a congregation deadens its faith for the sake of increased inclusiveness, it also deadens commitment. There is always the serious risk that the easier a congregation makes it for persons to belong, the more those persons may despise the congregation in the end. The church makes too many enemies for itself, and loses too many members, by its lax definition of what constitutes belonging.

Church councils need to constantly review their policies for persons joining the church and for persons being dropped from the church. They need to empathically consider spending money that will help reach out and accommodate persons who have previously been considered unapproachable or "not like us." They need to articulate to the world the community's central values, and they need to stand up for them. They and the congregation may need to look inward to begin accepting all that is common and dark inside them, so they might then be more accepting of others. We know to what we belong by knowing to what we do not belong. We know to what we belong by also knowing to what we all belong. Belonging is anchored for parishioners when the church council opens a congregation to new ways of being brother and sister with all people, while yet preserving the congregation's communal identity.

Mobilizing Hope

A church council ministers to persons when it helps mobilize hope in them. One simple, but profound, way the council can do this is by striving to keep parishioners active. Hope becomes mobilized in individuals and congregations when they become appropriately active.

Matthew records the incident of Jesus' meeting the paralytic man and laying upon him these two healing benedictions: "Take heart, son; your sins are forgiven. . . . Stand up, take your bed and go to your home" (Matt. 9:2, 6). We, like the paralytic, become able to act when we are filled with hope ("your sins are forgiven"). But we are also filled with hope when we begin to act ("stand up, take your bed"). Beginning to act is a therapeutic move to regaining our hope.

Life not only resumes but becomes gradually restored as hope-diminished parishioners become active. It is as if action embodies in itself the seeds of hope. Action generates a momentum, where one foot put in front of another propels the heart to take its own step. Like the paralytic, we are called to be mobile, for to begin to walk is to begin to find hope.

When a functional orientation subtly operates in a church's thinking, however, forced hopes may arise. For example, some churches are structured around the doing of projects. The activities of the churches sustain membership and relationships, rather than relationships sustaining activities. Consequently, when building projects are completed or membership drives are finished, these churches typically experience a let-down period. Without ongoing tasks to organize their energies and to bind the people together, these churches lapse into restlessness if not melancholy.

As a result, church councils may try to regain vitality by proposing projects that are not fitting for themselves or realistically achievable by their congregations. They may whip up a forced hope about what they can accomplish. This energetic insistence should not be interpreted as faith that "in God all things are possible." The impetus for this forced hope comes from the anxiety created when the churches' needs for continuously structuring activities are not fulfilled.

On the other hand, a functional orientation may give rise to a passive hope approach. If churches suffer disappointment when their grand projects are not achieved, or if they are unable to pick themselves up and put the machinery of planning back in operation again, church councils may then rely on a passive hope agenda. They hope that tomorrow things will be better, or they hope that things will change. This agenda is not a faithful "waiting upon the Lord." Passive hope, instead, functions as inactive activity. Such "activity" does not mobilize healthy hopes, however.

Church councils mobilize healthy hope by working to keep parishioners appropriately active. In general that will mean maintaining a vital ministry of activities for parishioners and encouraging participation in them. The message to be conveyed to parishioners is not that participation is an obligation, but that participation restores the soul—their own as well as others'.

The church council also works to keep itself from being swept away by the forced hopes of parishioners, and fortifies itself against charges that it is faithless or lacking in courage. Maintaining its equilibrium, the church council helps the congregation maintain appropriate boundaries on its activities and keeps before the congregation vital but realistic goals that can mobilize their hopes.

The church council may intercede on behalf of passive-hope parishioners by creating special activities for their participation. In addition, they may supply transportation, child care, meals, and other aids that will facilitate parishioners' becoming active again. At times the nature of the activity is not as crucial as the activity itself. Hope-diminished individuals just need to get moving again, even if that movement has no clear direction or is done half-heartedly. In varied ways, a church council can help paralytic members take up their beds and walk.

Finally, church councils give form and direction to parishioners' hopes by encouraging them to help with the birth of that which is ready to be born, and by encouraging them to impregnate social structures with seeds that will bring forth new births. In so doing, parishioners also become reborn, for each act is a begetting of their own hope. Blessed are those who stay mobile.

8.

CONGREGATIONAL LIFE THAT EMBRACES

Unlike the previous three chapters, the upcoming discussion about nurturing the relational life of the congregation is not linked one to one with the four central needs of parishioners: the needs to feel understood, to understand, to know one belongs, and to experience hope. But the centrality of those relational needs undergirds what is offered here. The following reflections on our worship life, service life, social life, and reconciling life are all specific attempts to help us be more intentional about encouraging a person-centered ministry within our congregations.

Worship Life

While there certainly is a place for formalism in the worship service, and for a spirit of decorum, formalism can sometimes alienate parishioners rather than nurture them. For example, pastors may fall into the habit of speaking to the congregation as if they were a third party: "The congregation is invited to sing the first three verses of the hymn." Do parishioners feel that it is their service, and that they are all one, when they are "invited" to participate in some way? And is it not rather distancing to speak to the congregation in this third-person way, "the congregation," rather than saying, "Let us sing the first three verses of our hymn"? Parishioners may become accustomed to formalism, but this does not justify the failure to bring a human touch to people's lives when it is possible.

Neither does a clipped, rote, and rushed liturgical style nurture a worshiping fellowship. Many Protestant clergy drone on with institutionalized words as if uttering them were the essence of the day. A holy place (the church) and holy words (the liturgy) do not a holy community make, although some clergy tend to think so. On the other hand, it may well be that pastors zip through services in monotone voices and with flabby clichés because they deeply sense that the services really are of limited spiritual importance to people.

Clergy and others can also become overly concerned with conducting a smooth service. Disturbances like a child's crying, or a speaker stumbling over words, or someone beginning to cough are taken as irritating interruptions. The service seems marred. The worshipful mood created seems lost, at least for a while. Indeed, for some laity and clergy there is a kind of anxiety that something "inappropriate" will happen during the service.

Parishioners themselves can become so tense about being a disruption in the service that they do not attend church at all. Fearful they might get a tickle in their throats, or that they might need to go to the restroom, or that they may get sick—even faint—keeps them from attending. And if they do attend, they do so with an underlying anxiety that diminishes the meaningfulness of worship.

I remember as a young boy feeling the solemnity of the service. When it started, it was as if something special was beginning that should go on uninterrupted, without the intrusion of anyone's personal needs. A transforming experience happened for me one Sunday, however. In the middle of the sermon the minister suddenly stopped. He just stood there, looking down for the longest time. He then began to sway slightly. All of that was frighteningly unexpected to me. I, along with others, sat there frozen.

But not my dad. He quickly jumped from his seat and ran to the pulpit, getting there just in time to catch the minister, who was collapsing from a heart attack. That greatly impressed me, both the pride in my father's ability to know what was going on as well as the realization that if *any* place and time should be most tender and caring for people it ought to be during worship. That was the beginning of my understanding that the service and its smoothness are not more important than people and their needs. Human need and being human are always more important than the formal ceremony. Cries and coughs and people leaving for personal reasons are no more disruptions to the smoothness of the service than are silent tears or wildly beating hearts, as long as we remind ourselves that in worship we are nothing more than a hurting crowd coming to Jesus.

The worship service also loses its human touch when it becomes jammed. Shoehorning a baptism, reception of new members, communion, and choir recognition into a normal service does not create a worshipful atmosphere. Necessary events get done, but often without a gentle pace that conveys to people that they are special and appreciated. Perfunctory strokes are often worse than no strokes at all.

Furthermore, services that "run over" can also erode the very uplifting of souls that worship hopes to accomplish. "Sometimes the service runs a half hour longer if we've got a lot to do," said one minister. This is not to say that his parishioners did not find those half hours meaningful. In many instances, however, the agenda is the pastor's rather than the people's. They begin to feel like a captive audience. Charity is also taxed as people coming for a second service cannot find a parking place, or those leaving late find their cars penned in. Consistent runovers lead to irritation at the organization of the church, and at the minister, who is thought to be insensitive. A line from an old hymn wisely counsels, "And let our ordered lives confess the beauty of thy peace." Our services need to express that order.

What clergy and lay leader does not have a story about the incredible behavior of some ushers? One pastor told of an usher who regularly thumbed through the checks while standing before the minister during the doxology. One layperson told of an usher who went down the side aisles with a clicker, counting people in the pews.

Ushers are often the first people parishioners and visitors meet when they come into the church. Ushers informally represent the congregation. More important, they have much to do with nurturing in others a feeling of being cared for and of belonging. Ushers should be taught the relational meaning of their role, not just the mechanics of their job. Ushering in a church is not like ushering in a theater. Ushering is not just for the functions of handing out bulletins and taking up the offering. Ushering is for welcoming people, for being an expression and extension of the love of God and the love of neighbor.

Ushers tend to think, however, that once they have fulfilled their job, they can mill around the back of the church during the service, or that they can go out to the kitchen for coffee. Milling behavior is disrespectful to parishioners, who find such activity distracting. It is also disrespectful to pastors, who must watch it all go on. Leaving the service is also discouraging to parishioners, who feel that who they are and what they are doing is not important enough for others (the ushers) to be a part of. Leaving is likewise discouraging to ministers, who feel that the word of faith they have come to proclaim is deemed unimportant to hear.

A case might also be made for ushers' not wearing a Sunday ushering uniform. When ushers are all dressed alike in colored coats and coordinated pants and/or skirts, this can smack too much of being at a "performance" where people are spectators. It also sets the ushers apart from the parishioners. The intent of worship, however, is to call us to remember that we are all one before God. Anything that contributes to the awareness that we stand as one people before our Creator should be embraced. Anything that detracts from that awareness stands in need of reevaluation.

Service Life

Giving to others is also at the heart of the crowd around Jesus. We are a servant people, called to nurture others as we have been nurtured.

Jesus instructs us about how to relate to others when we give to them. On the one hand he says, "When you give alms, do not let your left hand know what your right hand is doing" (Matt. 6:3). Forget yourself, Jesus is saying. He knew how self-righteous people can get in their giving. Parishioners as well as clergy can become pompous in their "caring." Rather than supporting and expressing the love of God, giving can become a kind of patronizing condescension. "Giving" becomes a handout. "Help" becomes charity. A "donation" becomes dole. That kind of giving neither creates human bonds with the person needing help nor brings maturity to the community who is "servicing" others.

Similarly, kindness can be a substitute for relating. A church might decide to open its basement two nights a week to the homeless. This is a kind act. But there is a difference between a church's making its facilities available to people and its making people a part of itself. Churches can be oblivious to the limits of their acceptance of others, especially when they can point to their kind acts toward those others. Ecclesiastical kindness frequently masks distancing, while parading itself as acceptance.

On the other hand, Jesus says, "Do to others as you would have them do to you" (Matt. 7:12). Think about how it would feel, Jesus is saying. He knew how people can become humble and understanding when they imagine themselves on the receiving end of help. If we realize that we would want others to still respect us as equals even if we were down and out, then we will bring that same "we're all in it together" attitude to our giving to others. If we give, but realize that we would be too proud ourselves to receive assistance, then we must own up to our subtle treatment of others as being less than ourselves. When we convey to those in need that we all are needy and vulnerable to setbacks, then our giving nourishes not only the body but the heart and soul as well. Then are genuine relationships formed and deepened. Then do we truly know that we are nothing more than a hurting and hoping crowd around Jesus. Those who consider themselves outside that circle are missing much.

Clergy and lay leaders do a disservice by pinching service from parishioners, however. Perhaps nothing drives parishioners away or dampens the spirit of a community more than feeling coerced. Coercion comes in a variety of forms: direct demanding of money or time from people, playing on their sympathies, infusing guilt in them, or subtly ridiculing them. The extracted "gift" may momentarily fill the collection plate, but it eventually empties the pew. Relationships are strengthened in the congregation when clergy and lay leaders consistently proclaim the true motivation for giving: We give out of gratitude and love for God, who first loved us. We give as a community who has known the faithfulness and forgiveness of our Creator. Giving, therefore, is not a duty; it is a joy. A cheerful giver is one who joins his or her neighbors in thanking God. The focus of stewardship drives, therefore, should not primarily be on eliciting funds from individual parishioners, but upon lifting up the memories of the congregation and encouraging the thankfulness of their hearts.

A special word should be said about the service of "caregivers" in the church. Professional caregivers are pastors, pastoral counselors, and persons with religious careers who by calling have dedicated their lives to the well-being of others.

Lay caregivers are those teachers, leaders, Stephen ministers, and other volunteers in the church who by faithful duty have committed themselves to helping parishioners and serving the parish. The crowd around Jesus is ordained to be a community of memory and mutual aid—a community caring for each other because they remember how they have been cared for. Caregiving blesses both those who extend care and those who receive it. Furthermore, in caring we participate with God in God's creating, sustaining, and redeeming work in the lives of each woman, man, and child. The essence of supportive relationships in the church rests in the willingness and capacity of the people to be empathic caregivers.

Caregiving can be draining, however. Caregivers can begin to lose a sense of well-being by overly caring, by trying to be too responsible and too helpful with people's needs. On the one hand, therefore, too much quantity leads to a loss of quality. That is, even when the most important tasks in life are constantly demanded of us, they lose their vitality. Ministers feel deeply moved at the outset of their careers when they share in the profound grief of parishioners. They feel special; they feel that they have witnessed holy moments. But eventually the constant need to respond to people's pain and anguish wears ministers down. The holy moments lose their glow. The sharing dissipates into a feeling of obligation. An excessive amount of caregiving results in the loss of the quality of meaning and satisfaction that a caregiving act inherently possesses.

Jesus knew this himself. However much compassion he had for the crowd around him, at times Jesus fled the people when their need completely exhausted him.

Ministers, however, often feel guilty for wishing people would leave them alone, and for feeling angry inside every time a person asks for one thing more. "How many hours a week do you generally spend at the church, at the hospital, at the funeral home, or in someone's home?" I may ask ministers when they come for therapy. "Oh, about sixty-plus hours a week," they may reply. "Well, it's little wonder that you're feeling irritable and empty. You've been giving, giving, giving week after week, and when someone asks you for more, and you haven't had a chance to be refilled yourself, you feel as you do." Ministers know this with their heads, but their consciences typically stay unimpressed. They still feel anxious and guilty. They think they should be immune to being drained by their caregiving. Quantity erodes quality, however.

On the other hand, a loss of quality leads to a feeling of too much quantity. That is, when caregiving activities create a great deal of anxiety in the caregiver, or generate depressive moods, then these activities seem to demand too much time, effort, or attention. Those caring acts a person wishes to avoid sap a significant amount of that person's energy; not energy that would be expended in the actual doing of the act, but energy expended in the constant dread of facing the act. A female Stephen minister, for example, may become ill at the thought of visiting a parishioner in the hospital who has recently undergone a mastectomy. The frightening thought that it might happen to her, and the worry about what she will say to the bereft woman, make the hospital visit an overwhelming task. When the quality of the caring act is filled with anxiety, loathing, or despondency, the quantitative amount of energy it consumes is enormous. As a result, the caregiver becomes emotionally, physically, and spiritually drained.

Jesus knew this, too. Although he always seemed to be undaunted by the type of caregiving required of him—lepers and wildly psychotic men reaching out to touch him did not scare him, for example—he, too, was overwhelmed by the ultimate caregiving request: to die so that others might live.

When caregivers are drained, their capacity for doing dwindles, as does joy in doing. Caring relationships with others continue, but the caregiver feels "pushed" to relate rather than "drawn" to relate. A normal desire to withdraw sets in, which is typically brushed aside as weakness, unfaithfulness, or selfishness. Caregivers press on, becoming ever more inwardly pressed. If the depletion of the caregiver continues, and/or the demands upon the caregiver continue unabated, then drained caregivers can become *at risk* caregivers. At risk means that caregivers can become susceptible to behavior that is damaging to themselves and to others. Increased pressure within caregivers, and greater expectations from those in the congregation, can lead a professional or lay caregiver to either "act in" (become inwardly depressed, resentful, or angry) or to "act out" (interact with others in inappropriate ways). One at risk pastor privately shared his secret cynicism, which had developed over the years: "Parishioners don't give a damn about you when they're hurting." An at risk lay caregiver acted out her frustration when she phoned all members in the congregation and told them how viciously the pastor had treated her.

Caregivers at risk are often unaware they are at risk. Manifestations of their anger, hostility, inappropriate behavior, or blaming others often are not visible to them. Even when directly confronted, at risk caregivers often disavow the meaning of their behavior.

When caregivers at risk relate with others, they do not generally aid the relationship; they injure it. Furthermore, when at risk caregivers interact with each other and with the congregation, the condition of the whole system worsens. Problems and conflicts within the church often arise from professional and lay caregivers who are at risk. There is nothing more nurturing of relationships in the church than faithful caregivers. Conversely, there is nothing more destructive to relationships in the church than at risk caregivers.[1]

We must keep this in mind as we talk about nurturing relationships within the church. First, caregivers must become wise about their limitations. They must let their heads dictate their actions even when their consciences prompt them to repeat debilitating ways. They must gradually learn to take care of themselves and to see that self-care is not selfishness but good sense. They must also learn that not only can they fail to be helpful to others as they become increasingly drained, but that they can also inadvertently hurt others as they become at risk caregivers. Taking care of oneself is not sinful. It is a personal and communal necessity.

Second, the congregation must strive to take care of its professional and lay caregivers. Ministers should be given adequate vacation periods, and they should be required to use them. Lay caregivers should be relieved by others from time to time and shown gratitude for all they do. All caregivers should be encouraged by the congregation to keep their spiritual life strong, for one of the first losses suffered by people drained by caring is the feeling of God's intimate presence with them.

Third, we in the church must be wise about ourselves as a community. Our thought might be that clergy, lay leaders, and congregations are basically healthy, and that the problems for which they need help are the exceptions. The truth, however, may be the reverse of this. Realistic appraisal suggests that dysfunction, disequilibrium, and the forces moving toward depletion may be more normative in the church than health. That condition need not be a despairing realization—just a painfully focusing one. Our good hope can keep us motivated to make the church and its people the means of grace they are intended to be. Our clear vision can keep us vigilant for those dark forces that pervert our community's memory and mutual aid.

Social Life

Eating together is sacramental in the church. In giving us the bread and wine, Jesus calls us to remember how finite each of us is and how much we need each other to make it through life. In seating us at his table, Jesus says to us, "I've come back after the Resurrection to be with you. You are not alone." In eating the Lord's Supper together, we are once again that intimate crowd around Jesus.

That same spirit can also infuse all the common acts of eating together in the church. Potlucks and church picnics, recognition suppers and wedding receptions, doughnuts at Bible studies and snacks with the youth can all be very humanizing and reassuring experiences for persons. Breaking bread together affirms our commonality (we are each a finite creature who must eat), affirms our common interdependence on each other (we depend on each other for the preparation, distribution, and purchasing of the food we eat), and affirms our common and ultimate reliance on God (who "gives us this day our daily bread").

Along with our eating together, there are other acts that can enrich relationships. Hugs, for example, can be warm expressions of care. Hugs bridge loneliness, show acceptance, help soothe fears, and even confirm our masculinity or femininity. Similarly, sharing life stories with one another, or sharing confessions, can help people feel understood and can lead them to find in the church a place where they more fully understand themselves. Then, too, getting our hands dirty together as we paint a room in the church or clean up the church lawn or pull out an old boiler can also bind us together.

Remember, however, to be wise in all of this. In the first place, not everyone has the same tolerance for connectedness. Some individuals panic at the thought of turning to their neighbor during worship, extending a hand, and saying the words "The Lord be with you." Potential visitors to churches are known to ask current members if that ritual is practiced, and, if it is, they decline to attend. While there is nothing wrong with this act of Christian greeting, it should not be assumed that it is automatically a strengthener of relationships.

Similarly, receiving or giving hugs is very difficult for some parishioners. Likewise, sharing one's story, let alone making a confession, is near impossible for others. To expect parishioners to shake hands or hug or share as a way of solidifying relationships is at times to accomplish the opposite—namely, to estrange them. People vary in how much connectedness they can tolerate.

In the second place, people vary in how much connectedness they need. Worshiping with others may be all the involvement and belonging that certain parishioners require. A planned community meal may be bypassed by some parishioners not because they are angry but because they are not hungry for companionship.

In the third place, we need to be "wise as serpents" (Matt. 10:16) in recognizing that expressions of friendship and care can be used for purposes other than enjoying and strengthening relationships. Encouraging others to come for a fellowship meal can be a way of buttering them up. "Let's invite all the stewardship captains and their spouses for a nice dinner here at the church, and then we'll do a number on them," said one functionally oriented minister. "That way they'll become the core of our giving base." Unfortunately, in the church eating together often aims toward some goal other than celebrating and deepening parish relationships. Similarly, a hug and "kiss of peace" can be for sexual excitement rather than for affectionate recognition. Urging others to tell about themselves can be a form of voyeurism rather than an invitation to share.

Nurturing relationships in the church, therefore, requires that clergy and lay leaders be empathic as well as shrewd. We should attempt to understand the varying relationship needs of others, as well as the varying intensity of those needs, and we must respond appropriately. Treating all people the same can be a lazy, one-size-fits-all approach that fails to respond to people as individuals.

At the same time, we should be worldly wise about people's motives. While we may respond to people as God's children, we must also remember that they all have feet of clay. Being shrewd means not becoming too depressed or disillusioned when others act selfishly. This is not a pessimistic stance; it is a tough-minded stance that keeps us from becoming hard-hearted. Being wise as a serpent keeps us from being Pollyannaish about our relationships. Being innocent as doves keeps us from being cynical about them.

The Reconciling Life

Beneath the obvious life of the church—its worship, service, and social involvements—beats another life: the church's reconciling life. Relationships are constantly being strained and relaxed, hurt and mended, broken and renewed. Parishioners expend tremendous energy attempting to overcome estrangements, to protect feelings, and to extract apologies. Cohesion within the community as a whole also fluctuates. At certain periods the community feels solidly united. At other times discontent shakes the foundation.

Reconciliation between people in the church often necessitates forgiving each other. We need to know how to appropriately forgive in the church, for that is one powerful means of healing relationships.

The importance of teaching and practicing forgiveness in the church can be challenged, however. In the story of the prodigal son, the son rehearses his confession, only to have his father brush it aside in the joy of having his lost son return. In this story, the act of asking for forgiveness and the act of forgiving are not made as important as the fact that a broken relationship is healed. And this is true, for the healing of relationships is the ultimate aim, no matter how it is brought about.

Difficulties arise, however, when no opportunity is given or allowed for people in the church to experience and practice forgiveness. When the hard work of forgiveness is avoided or minimized, we cheat ourselves and others out of a life-enhancing lesson. If we in the church make excuses for each other's behavior, or hide our hurt when we are injured, or offer a quick, superficial pardon, such as "It's okay; just don't do it again," we may deny each other the experience, the power, and the knowledge of forgiveness. Forgiveness is not just loving and accepting each other. It is not saving each other from guilty consciences when guilt is the appropriate feeling we should have. Acceptance without the boundaries that forgiveness calls for does not foster growth—it fosters selfishness; it does not strengthen relationships—it makes them shallow.

The same experience of reconciling forgiveness is also lost when it becomes a legalistic demand in the church. Some clergy and lay leaders, for instance, would have us believe that one is worthy only when one feels worthless, that one's highest aspiration should be to confess one's sinfulness and to throw oneself utterly into prayers for forgiveness. Such theological pounding fills many parishioners with empty despair rather than with love, leaving them dependent upon a vengeful God rather than rejoicing over the Creator's goodness. Congregations who pressure and demand public confessions by their members as a spiritual means of trying to beat the devil out of them often leave these persons feeling like hell. It is small wonder then that even the word *forgiveness* feels foreign, disgusting, or empty to many individuals. A sign outside a church read "Don't let your sins kill you. Let the church help." In spite of its best intentions, some forms of church life do kill rather than raise dead spirits when it comes to the matter of forgiveness.

Asking for forgiveness from others is no easy thing. It involves hurt. It involves an ability and willingness to confess our shortcomings, to feel the pain that one has caused another person, and to do something about it. It involves the recognition that new life comes not from oneself alone but from grace beyond oneself. Forgiveness in the Bible is not so concerned with sorrow and contrition as it is with changing one's life and staying righteous. The message is "Forget the breast beating and shape up!" Forgiveness is the recovering of strength and power in life and the reconciliation of relationships.

The act of forgiving is also not easy. Injured parishioners have to show that the cuts of others deeply hurt and troubled them, and that forgiveness is a difficult thing to offer honestly. In forgiving, one does not forget, but one does let go so that the fresh, bloody wound can heal into scar tissue. Furthermore, true forgiveness focuses not just on how one has been injured, but it focuses also on the injury to the one who asks for forgiveness. As one parishioner said about another parishioner, "I have begun to realize that he didn't do this just to me. He did it to himself as well."

It seems, ultimately, that we all are in it together. The good that we do blesses others as well as ourselves. The ill that we do breaks ourselves as well as others. There is no such thing as "autonomy," no reality called "independence." There is no clergy, lay leader, or parishioner who is a separate, private-rights, self-determining individual, unencumbered by duties to others or isolated from the support of others. We are all in it together.

People come to the church hoping to find that kinship community. It was so in the past; it is so now; and it will be so in the twenty-first century. People yearn for relationships that will assure them they are truly understood. They yearn for others who can help them understand. They yearn to feel as if they belong. They yearn for hope. To minister to these needs is to faithfully care for the crowd around Jesus.

THE LEADERS AROUND JESUS

Then Jesus called his disciples to him and said, "I have compassion for the crowd, because they have been with me now for three days and have nothing to eat; and I do not want to send them away hungry, for they might faint on the way." The disciples said to him, "Where are we to get enough bread in the desert to feed so great a crowd?" Jesus asked them, "How many loaves have you?" They said, "Seven, and a few small fish." Then ordering the crowd to sit down on the ground, he took the seven loaves and the fish; and after giving thanks he broke them and gave them to the disciples, and the disciples gave them to the crowds. And all of them ate and were filled. (Matt. 15:32-37)

Clergy and lay leaders are the helpmate disciples of Jesus. He calls us to service, and he shares with us his concerns for his people. Like those original leaders, we become confused at times. We begin to panic at the new, challenging tasks before us because we have no definite plan, no comfortable procedure to follow.

Ministry, however, is always a faith adventure rather than a functional exercise. As we church leaders prepare for the twenty-first century, we hopefully have learned that God in

Christ leads us in those moments of our lives that seem slightly out of control. Our ministering efforts can never claim to "be" the future, but they can claim to demonstrate the future; that is, they can be a witness to the continual unfolding of God's creative acts and of our creative responses. Certainty in the form of rigid ideas and functions should be our adversary. Faith as openness to Christ's call to new forms of service should be our guide.

What we church leaders have also learned, one hopes, is to embrace the crowd as Jesus did—as hungering people yearning for substance. People are sustained for their journey when in Christ's community they feel Christ's care. May our attempts to nurture relationships in the church be faithful expressions of that care, blessing all and pleasing God.

NOTES

Introduction

1. I use the term *people* to mean those who are interested in the church and those who are already members in the church. The relational needs apply to both. *People* and *parishioners* are often used interchangeably.

2. This concept comes from the seminal work of Lyle E. Schaller in his book *Assimilating New Members* (Nashville: Abingdon Press, 1978), p. 63.

3. In my pastoral counseling I work from a self-psychology perspective. Self-psychology is a relatively new clinical-theoretical approach, established by the late Heinz Kohut from his years of psychoanalytic work with patients. I and other colleagues have expanded his work for the field of pastoral counseling.

4. See George Gallup, Jr., "Six Spiritual Needs of Americans Today," *Fellowship in Prayer* 43, 4 (August 1991): 31-36.

5. For an extended discussion of Peck's impact, see Robert L. Randall, "The Road Peck Travels," *The Christian Century*, November 21, 1990, pp. 1101-1103.

2. Yearnings to Understand in the Church

1. This is a modification and expansion of H. Richard Niebuhr's famous definition in his book *The Purpose of the Church and Its Ministry* (New York: Harper and Bros., 1956), p. 31.

Notes

4. Yearnings for Hope in the Church

1. J. W. Goethe, *Wilhelm Meister* (London: Chapman & Hall, 1899), p. 282.

5. Preaching That Reaches Out

1. The importance of imagination in preaching is now widely recognized. For further help see, Thomas H. Troeger, *Imagining a Sermon* (Nashville: Abingdon Press, 1990); Paul Scott Wilson, *Imagination of the Heart* (Nashville: Abingdon Press, 1989).

6. Teaching That Connects

1. Martin E. Seligman has popularized the psychological term and theory called "learned helplessness." See his book *Helplessness: On Depression, Development, and Death* (San Francisco: W. H. Freeman, 1975).

8. Congregational Life That Embraces

1. Robert L. Randall, *Pastor and Parish: The Psychological Core of Ecclesiastical Conflicts* (New York: Human Sciences Press, Inc., 1988).

SELECTED
BIBLIOGRAPHY

Beker, J. Christian. *Suffering and Hope: The Biblical Vision and the Human Predicament*. Philadelphia: Fortress Press, 1987.

Fromm, Erich. *The Revolution of Hope Toward a Humanized Technology*. New York: Harper & Row, 1968.

Gallup, George, Jr. "Six Spiritual Needs of Americans Today." *Fellowship in Prayer* 43, 4 (August 1991): 31-36.

Harris, Maria. *Fashion Me a People: Curriculum in the Church*. Louisville, Ky: Westminster/John Knox Press, 1989.

Johnson, Barry L. *Choosing Hope*. Nashville: Abingdon Press, 1988.

Kohut, Heinz. *The Analysis of the Self*. New York: International Universities Press, Inc., 1971.

Moltmann, Jürgen. *Hope and Planning*. New York: Harper & Row, 1971.

Niebuhr, H. Richard. *The Purpose of the Church and Its Ministry*. New York: Harper and Bros., 1956.

Oswald, Roy M., and Speed B. Leas. *The Inviting Church: A Study of*

Selected Bibliography

New Member Assimilation. New York: The Alban Institute, 1987.

Paulus, Trina. *Hope for the Flowers.* New York: Paulist Press, 1972.

Randall, Robert L. *Pastor and Parish: The Psychological Core of Ecclesiastical Conflicts.* New York: Human Sciences Press, Inc., 1988.

_____. "The Road Peck Travels." *The Christian Century,* November 21, 1990, pp. 1101-1103.

Schaller, Lyle E. *Assimilating New Members.* Nashville: Abingdon Press, 1978.

Schaller, Lyle E., and Charles A. Tidwell. *Creative Church Administration.* Nashville: Abingdon Press, 1975.

Seligman, Martin E. *Helplessness: On Depression, Development, and Death.* San Francisco: W. H. Freeman, 1975.

Seymour, Jack L., and Donald E. Miller. *Contemporary Approaches of Christian Education.* Nashville: Abingdon Press, 1982.

_____. *Theological Approaches to Christian Education.* Nashville: Abingdon Press, 1990.

Stotland, Ezra. *The Psychology of Hope: An Integration of Experimental, Clinical, and Social Approaches.* San Francisco: Jossey-Bass, Inc., 1969.

Worley, Robert C. *A Gathering of Strangers: Understanding the Life of Your Church.* Philadelphia: The Westminster Press, 1976.

Zikmund, Barbara Brown. *Discovering the Church.* Philadelphia: The Westminster Press, 1983.